Contents

As India becomes a more robust global economy, most Indian jobs require candidates to have globally relevant skills like critical thinking, problem-solving, and self-management. A timely and must-read book by Senior Editor Economist, Mr Y. C. Halan, for all students and job aspirants looking to thrive professionally, whether in employment or entrepreneurship. An in-depth guidance on the most sought-after professional and personal skills that are essential in the ever-evolving global workspace.

—Alok Mehta
Journalist, TV broadcaster, writer,
and Padma Shri awardee

The 21st century requires very different skills compared to the 20th century for success. Lack of these skills is the prime reason for a large percentage of Indian youth being unemployable in spite of degrees and diplomas which were regarded as the passport to success in the earlier century. Lack of these skills also blocks the career growth of a large number of professionals in diverse domains. This book is for those who wish to equip themselves with 21st-century global skills to increase their chances of success in their chosen field whether they are at entry level or wish to move up in their careers. Also, this book is not for rapid reading. Readers are advised to follow a Read-Learn-Do-Repeat model for each step. It's important to practice each step continuously until it becomes a habit. Success is a habit after all.

—Rajiv Tewari
Former advertisement manager, *Indian Express*

In a world full of noise and confusing opinions, Dr Halan's book cuts to the basics, providing good sense and guidance to those looking to make a mark. *From 9 to Success* is a great primer on what really matters in the global professional ecosystem!

—Jaya Mohan
Journalist

From 9 to 9 Success

Mastering Skills for the Global Work Ecosystem

Y. C. Halan

HAY HOUSE

HAY HOUSE INDIA
New Delhi • London • Sydney
Carlsbad, California • New York City

Hay House Publishers (India) Pvt. Ltd.
Muskaan Complex, Plot No.3, B-2 Vasant Kunj, New Delhi-110 070, India
Hay House Inc., PO Box 5100, Carlsbad, CA 92018-5100, USA
Hay House UK, Ltd., The Sixth Floor, Watson House, 54 Baker Street, W1U 7BU, UK
Hay House Australia Pty Ltd., 18/36 Ralph St., Alexandria NSW 2015, Australia

Email: contact@hayhouse.co.in
www.hayhouse.co.in

ISBN 978-81-19554-30-0
ISBN 978-81-19554-59-1 (ebook)

Printed at Repro India Limited

Dedication

To Mridula, who has been the source of motivation, inspiration, and guidance for sixty years.

Chapter One

INTRODUCTION

Essentials of Global Skills

'Would you be able to adjust in the glamourous corporate world with your family background?' I asked Anup Gupta who was appearing for an admission at a prestigious business institute in Hyderabad.

'No doubt, sir. Though my father is a peon and mother a domestic help, I am sure I will be able to adjust and rise to senior positions in any corporate entity, national or multinational,' replied the confident boy.

'How you are so sure?' asked the Dean.

'Because with the same family background, I could get admission in one of the most prestigious colleges of the University of Delhi,' replied Anup.

'We appreciate your confidence and wish you the best,' I said, indicating that the interview was over.

Anup topped the list of selected candidates and during his two-year stay at the institute, he impressed everyone with his intelligence, passion, and diligence. His greatest skill was his emotional involvement in the institute, his work, and his care for fellow students. When placement teams came for selection, he was the first to be selected by a prestigious multinational company. In the next twenty-three years, Anup moved up very fast in the company and had many headhunters running after him.

The next time I met Anup, he had become the CEO of a multinational company. He spent an hour with me during which I explored his work style, work strategy, and skills he developed to be in the superfast lane. I found that he had all those skills that multinational companies require from their CEO. These are known as 'global skills.' Let's explore this further.

In the 21st century, economies and workplaces are developing at an enormous and unbelievable rate. Changes in technology, the internet, and global competition have shown that the 21st-century economy is vastly different from the economies of earlier centuries, creating a new set of opportunities and careers that could never have been imagined and a new class of professionals which are entirely different from the previous eras.

This new work system is throwing new challenges at the management, managers, and workers. Also, economies have become global and multi-faceted and require managers to work in a high-performance culture and operate with greater autonomy and accountability. Therefore, to succeed in such a culture requires a new set of skills.

Unfortunately, youngsters aspiring for managerial roles are still having a 20th-century psyche and are not aware of the new globalisation requirements. This is creating a remarkable difference between the perceptions of students and their potential employers. A study by the Association of American Colleges and Universities concluded that while a majority of employers sought communication, collecting and evaluating information, and the ability to solve complex problems in the persons they were recruiting, less than 30 per cent of college students realised that these soft skills were essential to their success. Thus, we can see that new economic opportunities have ushered in a high level of competitiveness and the success of a manager depends on acquiring more relevant and contemporary skills.

Also, the fast expansion of the corporate sector in the 21st century has had a significant effect on people, economies, societies, and workplaces. Development in technology has led to a new set of careers, which are becoming more popular. These include fields of biotechnology, laser, robotics, information technology, telecommunications, information management, computer, aerospace, medical, and superconductivity technology. Self-employment and small business developments have also become popular.

Governments in the US and Europe have realised this and have designed policies to equip students with new skills. The United States was the first to do that, followed by Canada, the UK, and New Zealand. International organisations like APEC and the OECD helped them in this process. Unfortunately, India failed to do so and, therefore, the majority of Indian graduates are still not aware of global skills that are demanded by global (multinational) companies. And despite having the largest English-speaking, intelligent, and innovative population in the world, India was unsuccessful in adapting to this new work structure and reaping the benefits of its demographic dividend because Indian leaders failed to realise that the growth and fruition of the younger population were not possible with old and out-dated skills.

Also, though Indians from a few reputed institutes are getting high-paying jobs from global companies, the majority of the educated Indian youth is missing this opportunity because business schools are not equipping them with global skills. Consequently, not even ten per cent of management graduates are employable in the corporate sector. Due to this reason, many MBA students have to opt for lower-quality jobs.

Thus, after considering all factors, the involvement of everyone—employers, trainers, unions, workers, and the government—is necessary to build the nation's progress. And most importantly, dynamic partnerships are required to ensure that all youngsters acquire skills that 21st-century economies require. The economic health of the company and an individual's well-being rests on the success of this.

What Are Global Skills?

During the last few decades, India has been changing at an accelerating pace, which in turn, has led to new work models and skills. And though business schools should develop these skills, they have not been doing it because most of them are not aware of global skills and their importance in the career growth of students. Therefore, students themselves should develop these skills in order to progress professionally.

But what are global skills? Simply put, these are high-order skills, abilities, and learning dispositions required for success in global societies and workplaces and enable individuals to thrive in an international, multicultural, and rapidly changing environment. These skills are not only essential for success in a globalised workforce but also for effective citizenship in a world where borders are increasingly porous, and cultural diversity is celebrated.

Conclusion

The 21st century is witnessing significant developments in all business sectors, bringing important changes in the economy and workplace. It has also led to completely new categories of vocations. These new forms of corporate roles and work environments require a new set of skills. Not only that, but economies have also become global and extremely complex, making it necessary for the present generation to respond by acquiring new skills. Though business schools in the developed countries are giving high priority to developing these skills, the Indian business schools have not followed them. Therefore, students have to make efforts to develop these skills. The book is an attempt to educate them on how they can develop these skills.

Chapter Two

The Changing Corporate World

The corporate world is changing fast and has become more complex where the old hierarchical model of leadership doesn't work anymore. The 21st-century corporate system, being more volatile and uncertain, requires more dispersed controls and leadership through networking. The old system of the CEO making every decision no longer exists because one person cannot sift through tons of data regarding the company's performance, industry, economic environment, and competitors. Also, he has no time to disseminate the right information to the right people in real-time.

As for the workers in the 21st-century corporate culture, they no longer sweat away using old technological tools. They no more work on typewriters and written paper memos are as old-fashioned as a horse-drawn carriage. Modern technology has revolutionised 21st-century work organisations. Therefore, modern managers and workers have to learn how to use new technology in order to become more productive and successful.

All in all, the corporate world has completely changed. It has become ferociously ruthless, highly competitive, and extremely demanding. However, the reason why many people with high aspirations wish to join this world is because it ensures high rewards, a satisfying career, and an opportunity to develop rare skills. Let us take an in-depth look at these points.

1. **Fiercely Ruthless**

   The corporate world is extremely ruthless and those working have to face numerous challenges in a demanding environment. Besides satisfying the boss, you have to prove that you are liked by your peers. Besides working with others, you also have to protect your interests. If unable to prove your competence, your rivals will force you to quit.

2. **Highly Competitive**

   With markets becoming global, competition has become a strong market force. And since India was a socialist society before 1991, it lacked a competitive market and so many inefficient companies survived. But today, Indian markets are as competitive as the American markets, and companies that cannot face tough competition are eased out. In this scenario, you have to become highly competitive and only then you can move up on the executive ladder.

3. **Extremely Demanding**

   Every company, functioning in a cut-throat competitive environment, has to provide quality goods and services at low prices, strive hard to increase its market share, and keep the customer satisfied. These market compulsions are the reason why the corporate world constantly seeks and demands higher quality work and increased productivity. It is natural, therefore, that 'deliver or perish' is the catchphrase for managers. Those who perform excellently move up fast and those who fail are shown the door.

How to Prepare

If you want to be a corporate leader, you are expected to be a front-runner, an innovator, a dynamic motivator, a stern but fair judge, a diplomat, a politician, and a protector. You should be able to get along with different people, work hard, wear the right clothes, have the right friends, and possess congenial personalities. Power flows from attainment and to be an achiever, you have to develop five attributes in your personality. These are:

1. **Courage** to speak in a diplomatic and articulated way.
2. **Conviction** to believe what you say and make others believe that you are speaking intelligently.
3. **Clarity** in what you think and conveying it in an understandable language. You should be able to explain complicated things in the simplest words.
4. **Credibility** of the highest order to enjoy the trust of the bosses, colleagues, and clients.
5. **Wisdom** to make good decisions.

What Is Global Personality?

Global personality, in simple words, is a package of qualities and skills required in a person that distinguishes him from others. It is the totality of an individual's behaviour and emotional characteristics. Some of the important attributes that go into making a global personality are:

1. **Physical fitness**

   It is important to be physically fit as this aspect of life forms the foundation of both personal and professional success. Eating nutritious food, having a balanced diet, and exercising form the three pillars of a healthy lifestyle. Your daily intake should include half a plate full of vegetables and fruits, healthy proteins, such as fish, poultry, eggs, nuts, and beans, and carbohydrates from whole grains sources, such as oatmeal, whole wheat bread, and brown rice, and healthy fats and oils like olive and vegetable oils. You should also eat 'super foods' that provide excellent nutritional benefits by delivering extra energy, antioxidants, calcium, and heart-healthy fats and proteins to your body. This includes foods such as dried fruits, sweet potatoes, and bananas that provide complex carbohydrates which help to efficiently store and use energy, broccoli and other green vegetables, tomatoes, blueberries, and cocoa that contain antioxidants which remove cell-damaging free radicals from your blood, and milk which provides calcium to ensure healthy bones.

2. **Temperament**

   Since your decisions are influenced by your emotions, your success depends on your ability to understand and interpret them and respond in a sensitive, cool, and balanced manner. Thus, it is vital to understand the relation between your emotions and the decisions you make.

When you want to make a decision, you feel an emotion in your brain and your nervous system responds to it by creating feelings in your body, which is also called a gut feeling. Since emotions appraise and summarise an experience and accordingly inform your actions, a large number of your decisions get a hint from your emotional responses. This is a good thing because rather than leading a mechanical life, you are motivated by your feelings and emotions. However, you should not become a victim of those emotions. Many times, you are guided by your temporary feelings when it comes to taking a decision, which you may regret later because the decision may harm your interests. But by focusing your thoughts, you can control your feelings.

Another important point to note here is that though emotions are not well thought-out and clear-cut, their speed and utility make up for their deficiency in smoothness and accuracy. In fact, logical and cogent inconsistent emotions provide information simply and quickly as they tell you if a situation is the best for you. Suppose you are bargaining a deal and feel that something is amiss. This is actually your emotional system warning you to further think about the deal. Mary Lamia, a clinical psychologist and professor at the Wright Institute in Berkeley, California, states, 'Emotions can tell you something about the world that you may not have accurately perceived in another way. They are something to interpret and use rather than an annoyance that you should ignore or control. Just like the thumb on your hand, emotions have evolved to help you, even though at times they may seem to get in the way.'

3. **Resilience**

Confucius, whose thoughts greatly influenced China and other East Asian countries, more than 25 centuries back, believed that the 'green reed which bends in the wind is stronger than the mighty oak which breaks in a storm.' The events during the last two decades, marked by rapid and extreme swings, from boom to recession and back again, have proved that he was right. During the 2008-2018 period, when most countries were facing difficult economic times, India rose as a more resilient nation as the impact of the recession on its economy was minimal when compared to other prominent economies of the world including Russia and Mexico, which were hit severely, according to a report by The Carnegie Endowment for International Peace, which is a foreign-policy think tank.

The fact is that what can be said about economies also holds true for individuals. Resilient people prosper and grow fast as compared to those who become cynical in times of crisis because resilience gives them the ability to adapt to adverse circumstances. And though not everyone is born resilient, like most skills, resilience can be learnt.

Given below are some ways to become more resilient:

i. Build a family and social-emotional safety net as relatives and friends help in critical times. In the absence of this safety net, the most stable and secure people can break when faced with a crisis. An interpersonal safety network can be built by networking because the wider your network is, the safer you will be.
ii. Keep yourself healthy because physical fitness makes achieving resiliency easier. Studies show that a healthy lifestyle and emotional well-being help to manage and mitigate distress. Becoming healthy does not mean doing endless hours of exercise every day. The best way to keep fit is to eat fresh, home-cooked food, get eight hours of sleep, and go for regular walks. It keeps your body and your mind healthy, which, in turn, will lead to more resilience.
iii. Remain positive by cultivating a cheerful and positive attitude by being aware of your thoughts and curbing negativity before it begins.

Keep learning new skills, new techniques, and from mistakes so that your skills and knowledge remain fresh.

4. Leadership

A leader is a person who motivates others to act, guides them, and helps the team to adapt to change. Also, a leader is different from a manager.

A leader gives a new direction or vision to a group, while a manager controls or directs people and resources according to principles or values that have already been established. The manager uses a formal, rational method whilst the leader uses passion and inspires others.

Jack Welch exhibited leadership qualities as chief executive officer (CEO) of General Electric Co. from 1981 to 2001. He played an integral part in 600 acquisitions in emerging markets and increased GE's market value from $12 billion to $505 billion by the time he retired. In a fast-changing world, Welch insisted everyone at GE to welcome change and motivated them to continuously reinvent themselves and their work.

There are five qualities that a leader needs to develop in order to guide diverse teams successfully, promote collaboration, and drive the achievement of organisational objectives. Let us understand these five attributes:

1. **Authenticity**

   Though leadership in the 21st century has become more important than ever before, authentic leaders are in short supply. Therefore, those joining the corporate sector should be highly authentic, genuine, self-aware, and transparent to inspire loyalty and trust in those working with them. Leaders with high authenticity will always be in greater demand. The idea of authentic leadership is not new and has its origins in the Ancient Greek philosophy which considered authenticity an important trait to enable a person to control his destiny. The idea of authentic leadership was further developed by Bill George in his book, *Authentic Leadership*, which tried to substantiate that despite other important leadership skills, being trustworthy is the most important criterion.

2. **Reliability**

   A reliable leader is considered genuine, self-aware, and transparent and is able to inspire loyalty and trust in team members. Such leaders work with their own value system and always follow it. They are valued by employers because they are highly dependable and show consistently excellent results over long periods.

3. **Vision**

   A committed leader has to have a vision which implies that he needs to have the capability to analyse the present and think of the future. A leader's vision should not be limited only to the mission of the company, but it should also reflect in his actions, beliefs, and values. Another reason why having a long-term vision is important is because it provides the leader with a purpose to keep pushing on and a goal that needs to be realised. As suggested by Henry Adams, an American historian, those who aspire to be leaders must have the personality like the commander of a ship who 'must have a helm to grasp, a course to steer, a port to seek' so that the corporate ship sails on a right course.

4. **Willpower**

Willpower is an indispensable trait for an organisational leader. In the complex and ever-evolving landscape of business, leaders often face daunting challenges, unexpected setbacks, and the need to make tough decisions. Willpower acts as the driving force that propels leaders forward, even in the face of adversity. It enables them to stay focused on long-term objectives, maintain discipline in their actions, and resist distractions or temptations that could derail progress. Moreover, willpower sets an example for the entire organisation. When leaders exhibit self-control and determination, it inspires and motivates their teams to do the same. It fosters a culture of perseverance, resilience, and commitment to excellence. Ultimately, a leader's willpower is not just a personal attribute; it becomes a cornerstone of the organisation's success, guiding it through challenges and uncertainties while steering it toward its goals and aspirations.

5. **Wisdom**

Wisdom is a priceless asset for an organisational leader, transcending mere knowledge and experience. It involves the ability to apply discernment, sound judgment, and a deep understanding of human behaviour and complex situations. Wise leaders make well-informed decisions that consider both short-term goals and long-term consequences. They draw upon their experiences to navigate challenges, but they also recognise the value of continuous learning and adaptation. Wisdom allows leaders to remain calm and composed under pressure, inspiring confidence in their teams and stakeholders. Furthermore, it fosters empathy and compassion, enabling leaders to connect with employees on a personal level and make decisions that consider the well-being of all involved. In essence, wisdom is the compassion that guides leaders through the complexities of modern business, helping them chart a course that not only achieves organisational success but also upholds ethical values and sustains a positive organizational culture.

6. **Practical Skills**

Practical skills are of paramount importance for an organizational leader, as they bridge the gap between conceptual knowledge and effective implementation. While visionary thinking and strategic planning are vital, practical skills are what enable a leader to turn those visions into tangible results. These skills encompass a wide range of abilities, including project management, problem-solving, delegation, and time management. Practical skills allow a leader to set clear goals, develop actionable plans, and efficiently allocate resources to achieve objectives. They also empower leaders to address challenges as they arise, ensuring that the organization remains agile and adaptable in a dynamic business environment. Furthermore, practical skills in communication and team management facilitate effective collaboration and motivate teams to perform at their best. In essence, practical skills are the tools that transform a leader's vision into reality, driving the organisation toward success while fostering productivity, innovation, and accountability throughout the team.

Conclusion

In the ever-evolving landscape of the corporate world, adaptability and continuous improvement have emerged as the keys to professional success. As we conclude this chapter, we find ourselves at the intersection of change and opportunity, where the need to stay at the top of our game has never been more pronounced. The shifting dynamics of business, driven by technological advancements, globalisation, and the demand for innovation, necessitate a new paradigm of professional excellence.

The message is clear: the pursuit of professional success is not a one-time endeavour but a lifelong commitment to growth and development. The changing corporate world demands that we embrace a growth mindset—a mindset that recognises that our skills, knowledge, and abilities are not fixed, but malleable. It is a mindset that thrives on challenges, learns from failures, and continually seeks to enhance one's capabilities.

One of the central themes explored in this chapter is the importance of cultivating a diverse skill set. While domain-specific expertise remains crucial, the value of soft skills such as adaptability, communication, emotional intelligence, and leadership cannot be underestimated. These skills not only enhance our ability to excel in our respective fields but also empower us to navigate the complexities of human interaction and collaboration in a globalised world.

Furthermore, our exploration has illuminated the significance of staying attuned to industry trends and emerging technologies. In the digital age, where the pace of change is relentless, staying informed and being proactive in acquiring new knowledge is the cornerstone of professional success.

In closing, the changing corporate world beckons us to embrace the evolving landscape, recognising that change brings opportunity. To achieve and sustain professional success, we must remain agile, adapt to new challenges, and continuously refine our skills. The journey is not without its trials, but it is through these trials that we forge our path to excellence. In the chapters that follow, we will delve deeper into the specific skills, strategies, and insights required to thrive in this dynamic corporate environment. Each page turned will bring us closer to mastering the art of professional success in the changing world of business. As we embark on this journey, remember that the pursuit of excellence is not just about reaching the top—it's about soaring to new heights, setting new standards, and leaving a lasting impact on the world of business and beyond.

Chapter Three

Communication Skills

We all know that good communication skill allows us to deliver information quickly and accurately as well as create an impact. On the contrary, mediocre communication skills will always end in misunderstanding and frustration for all the parties involved. This is the reason that the ability to communicate effectively should be honed and developed as it can be highly beneficial for your professional as well as personal life.

Let's look at the following story that shows how one can solve difficult problems if one possesses the right communication skills.

Birbal is known for his wit and wisdom, but a trait of his which is usually overlooked is that he was also a great communicator and could articulate his message in an effective way.

Once a group of people complained to Emperor Akbar that their neighbours were eating puris (fried bread) every night when they were only eating rotis (bread baked on a pan). Akbar banned puris on the principle of equality. The neighbours, saddened by this verdict, went to Birbal who assured them that he would take care of the matter.

The next day, Birbal, while discussing state matters with Akbar, raised the puris' issue.

'What is wrong?' Why can't they eat rotis like others?' queried Akbar.

'They can, but your majesty, can they eat rotis with ghee (refined butter) on it?' Birbal replied with a question of his own.

'Yes, they can,' replied Akbar.

'So merciful, your majesty! Sir, do they also have the permit to apply ghee when baking on *tava* (pan)?'

'Yes!'

'And can they apply ghee on both sides of the bread as well?'

'Don't ask silly questions; they can,' stated Akhbar.

Thereafter, the neighbours were able to eat parathas (shallow-fried bread) every night for dinner.

***

What Is Implied by Good/Effective Communication Skills?

As discussed, communication skill plays a crucial role when it comes to achieving success in life. Bill Clinton, former president of the United States, owes much of his success to his communication skills. He was always able to put his point across despite his southern drawl. Nick Morgan, an American speaking coach, told in an interview with the Public Affairs Council that when Bill spoke, the room came alive. Winston Churchill, one of the most popular leaders of the 20th century, gave people hope during the Second World War by forming an emotional connection with them. Martin Luther King Jr., another top-grade communicator, was able to touch the hearts of people and beckon change through his impassioned and beautiful messages. Oprah Winfrey, also known as 'Queen of All Media', was the richest African American of the 20th century and North America's first black multi-billionaire and one of her biggest assets was that he was an excellent communicator.

Thus, we can see that effective communication is a tool that can open up a vast range of gateways. By studying other master communicators, you too can learn to successfully get your point across and achieve the desired goal whether you are talking to your family, conducting a board meeting, or running for an office.

But what do we mean by effective communication? In a nutshell, effective communication doesn't mean simply sharing information. Rather, it is an interaction between two or more persons to successfully give out, receive, and understand a message successfully. And many times, it is this transference and interpretation of a message that can make or break an important deal. The following story encapsulates this.

Jack and Max are walking from the church after the service. Jack wonders whether it is permissible to smoke while praying and asked Max. Max replied, 'Why don't you ask the priest?'

Jack approached the priest and asked, 'Father, can I smoke while I pray?'

The father replied, 'No, my son, you should not because smocking is disrespect to God.'

Jack returned and told Max about the priest's reply. Max told Jack that he had phrased the question in the wrong way.

Max then went to the priest and asked, 'Father, can I pray while I smoke?'

The Priest replied, 'By all means, my son.'

The story conveys that intelligent communication can be the factor that turns disappointment into accomplishment and vice versa.

Developing Communication Skills

The aspect of good communication takes an even more significant role in the business world. All corporate entities prefer those who can communicate clearly and positively. Thus, in today's competitive jobs market, it is an important skill to develop as it has now become the main element for corporate success.

As covered earlier, communication skill is an interpersonal ability enabling you to express and articulate your thoughts, clearly and concisely. But many people think that effective communication just entails the way you use words. The truth is that to communicate effectively, it requires many other abilities, such as non-verbal communication, the ability to understand your own emotions as well as that of others, active listening, speaking animatedly, etc. But broadly speaking, we can say that effective communication has three components: active listening, effective speaking, and strategising communication. We will cover these components separately and also look at how we can develop the same through thoughtful efforts.

Active Listening

Active listening is an invaluable tool for facilitating effective communication. It is a communication technique that involves listening with full attention to what is being said.

Yet, most of us believe that communication is only

speaking and that is the reason why many people keep on speaking non-stop, without listening to the other person. In fact, a good communicator will always first listen intently and carefully before responding properly.

An important point to note here is that listening is not the same as hearing. Listening involves trying to genuinely see the other person's point of view and understand what the other person is trying to communicate. The following anecdote elucidates the same:

> A person went to his bank and withdrew 50,000 rupees. After a few minutes, he returned to the cash counter and said to the cashier, 'When I counted the notes in the car, I found . . .'
>
> 'But we are not responsible after you have left the counter. It is written here. I can't do anything.'
>
> 'Okay. However, I wanted to tell you that it was 55,000,' said the customer and then quietly walked out.

How to Be a Good Listener?

Most people are impatient listeners and just want to continue with their narration without giving a chance to the other person to provide his version. Though it might sound easy to understand, there is a lot more to this technique. Following are four fundamentals to keep in mind in order to become a good listener:

Eye Contact

'Our eyes are the window to the soul' is a true axiom as eyes can express our emotions even when words fail. Therefore, eye contact is very important during communication as it allows you to communicate your thoughts and feelings and also enables you to develop a connection with the person you are speaking to. Not making eye contact may convey that you are not interested in what the other person is saying. All great orators are well aware of this as they know that listening happens as much with the eyes as with the ears.

Therefore, you should develop the habit of making good eye contact. Maintaining eye contact is essential to make the other person feel that he is being listened to carefully. Studies have shown that people who make better eye contact are thought to be more warm, attractive, honest, and confident. It also gives the impression that they are powerful and emotionally stable.

In short, good eye contact makes you popular with persons you interact with because it imparts a sense of intimacy in your exchanges, leaving the listener more positive about you. It also increases the quality of your face-to-face interactions because when you make eye contact with the individuals in the audience, you are able to make a personal connection with them which translates to better networking. Also, active and positive eye contact helps you focus and concentrate on the topic of discussion. The moment you lose the eye contact, your mind wavers, breaking the flow of the discussion.

Improving Eye Contact

Though it takes a little practice to be able to confidently hold eye contact, it can be strengthened. Following are suggestions to achieve the same:

Maintain the Right Balance

Balancing curiosity and appropriateness is important to achieve effective eye contact. It becomes awkward if you don't maintain a balance and stare at the person, making him or her uncomfortable. Too much eye contact can also become intruding for the other person. The following are some guidelines to keep in mind:

1. When others are speaking to you, good eye contact is important as it shows that you're listening intently and are interested in what they are saying. However, you should never stare at them while they are speaking. Overdoing eye contact can be counter-productive, so, maintain a healthy balance by keeping the eye contact for five to ten seconds and then focusing on something else. It will also help you to gather your thoughts and comprehend the conversation before re-establishing eye contact.
2. Do not show your anxiety and nervousness, particularly if you are not used to maintaining eye contact while speaking. You can overcome uneasiness by gradually increasing the duration of eye contact. Begin with a shorter eye contact duration and gradually increase it as per your comfort level. Also, do not hasten to make this increase; take your time and increase it at a pace that feels natural.

3. Regular practice will help you improve your eye contact technique. Start with your family members and then include friends. You can also practise in front of a mirror. It is the most effective technique to improve your eye contact skills. Also, watch news anchors on the TV as they are experts in maintaining a healthy ratio between eye contact and looking shortly away.

Do Not Interrupt

Another good habit to inculcate is to not interrupt others during conversations, especially when they are trying to make an important point. Being a chronic interrupter can also endanger your relationship with the person as no one likes to be disturbed when they are speaking. Also, consistent interruptions not only indicate a lack of respect for the speaker but can make the other person feel that he or she is insignificant. Anneli Blundell, an interpersonal intelligence expert, says, 'A good conversation is like a game of tennis. You take turns. The pace might speed up or slow down, but you still take turns. Your partner on the court doesn't serve seven tennis balls in a row and expects you to keep them all in play. They don't return your serve and then serve another ball when the previous ball is still in play. It's one ball, one at a time, back and forth. Just like a good conversation.'

Now let's look at the scenario where we are on the receiving end, i.e., we are being interrupted by someone. An important thing to keep in mind is that though constant interruption during a conversation is obstructive, we should never take interruption personally. There could be many trivial reasons for the interruption such as the interrupter's brain may be working on overdrive or he may be excited to make his point. 'Sometimes they have gotten enough information from the speaker and want to engage in debate or conversation by saying what they are thinking. Sometimes they [may even] think you are done talking, so you consider it interrupting but they don't,' says Banks Cohn, founder and president of ADRA Change Architects.

But if you find yourself being constantly interrupted by someone, you can try the following techniques:

1. Politely ask the person that you will answer all the queries after you have finished. Laura Rose, who is the global marketing director at Stanley Security, provides a great way to word this sentiment in order to stop the potential interrupters and it is as follows: 'There are a lot of different pieces to this explanation, so please bear with me. I want to tell you the entire story. Then I want us to wrap around and get your thoughts on specific details.' The importance of replying politely and in a lowered voice is well captured by Kevin Sensenig, vice president of learning and development with Dale Carnegie Training. He says, 'By lowering your voice slightly, keeping an even pace, and confidently continuing to make your statement, you can disarm the interrupter . . . Continue speaking until the other person stops, and move directly to your main point.'

2. Do not stop when interrupted and instead, keep on talking, ignoring the interrupter's effort to butt in. Though this may lead to some confusion as both of you would be talking simultaneously, the interrupter would understand that you would not allow him to take the floor and he would soon give in.

Body Language

Let's study the following example. In a classroom, students were making a lot of noise. Then a teacher entered the classroom. He walked straight to the table, looked around, turned around, and then started writing on the blackboard a question on the topic he had taught yesterday. All the noise stopped and the class was dead silent. Students now sat straight and nervous. They realised that an answer would be expected of them at any moment.

The teacher looked around and looked at one boy. The boy stood up, but the teacher shifted his gaze to a girl sitting next to the boy. The girl began to answer the question, but the teacher once again looked away and the girl stopped halfway. Now the teacher looked at another boy sitting near the window. He stood up and started answering. The teacher then dropped his shoulders and sighed. This gesture of the teacher was enough to communicate that he wasn't happy with the answer and this was clearly understood by other students, who immediately raised their hands for permission to give the answer. How the teacher was able to get so many responses and all those different reactions without uttering a single word? The answer is: through the power of body language.

Body language can be defined as non-verbal communication where messages are sent through postures and eye-contacts instead of spoken words. It has become a highly sought-after attribute in today's competitive world. All good companies give high priority to people with good body language because it helps in getting deals finalised and bringing profits to the company.

Your body language, which includes body movements, facial expressions, vocal tone, and volume, reveals what you are actually feeling and thinking, even if you are consciously aware of these developments. Hence, it plays a crucial role in negotiations because if your body language does not support what you are saying, you may lose the deal. Not only that but good negotiators are also proficient in judging every movement of the body and therefore, have an immense advantage while communicating with others. Thus, if you also are good at reading body language, you would be an asset to the company.

When properly used, body language can be your key to greater success. Following are a few suggestions for optimising your body language to project confidence, credibility, and your personal brand of magnetism:

1. The way you stand is important. Always stand erect as it would enhance your confidence level. Keep your shoulders back and head high to look more powerful and assured to those who are seated. Also, don't just stand in one place and instead, move around. When you are sitting, keep your both feet flat on the floor and your

arms away from your body. You can also spread your belongings on the table to claim more territory and look more confident.

2. While standing, keep your two feet away from each other. The reason being that standing with closed feet indicates uncertainty. With feet apart, you will look firmer and more assertive. Keep your knees at ease and centralise your weight on the lower part of your body.
3. When speaking, keep the pitch of your low because speaking at a high pitch will show you to be less tolerant, weak, and more edgy. To speak in a soft pitch, put your lips together and say, 'Um hum, um hum, um hum.' This exercise will bring out the finest tone of your voice.
4. Maintain a positive eye contact with the person you are talking to. Do not be shy because businessmen from developed countries expect eye contact during a conversation.
5. Use both hands to show gestures to support what you are saying because hand gestures are linked to speech and therefore, your hand movements will energise your thinking. Simply put, hand gestures help improve the verbal content and make the speaker seem more certain.
6. Keep your movements relaxed to show your credibility and truthfulness. Showing both palms of your hands will indicate that you are not hiding anything. It will make you more persuasive and cast you in a positive light. Also, keep your arms at waist level as this will make you look like a confident and reliable person.

7. Adopt steepling—tips of your fingers touching with palms separated—as it will give an indication that you are quite certain about the point you are making. The steepling technique should be used when you want to project conviction and sincerity about a point you are making.
8. Do not use nervous gestures like rubbing your hands together, bouncing your feet, drumming your fingers on the desk, or playing with your jewellery or with your hair. If you feel tense, take a deep breath and steady yourself by placing your feet firmly on the floor and your hands, palm down, on your lap or the table. This will indicate that you are calm and confident.
9. Keep smiling because it has a powerful effect and everyone likes happy faces. It will also amplify your sense of security and help communicate to others your trustworthiness. A study conducted by Duke University shows that a smile changes the other person's emotional state in a positive way and we remember those who smile at us.
10. A handshake is more than a simple gesture to build connections. You should always give a warm-hearted handshake. A good handshake is a powerful tool when it comes to cultivating a bond and leaving a lasting impression. Avoid 'dead fish' and 'bone-crusher' handshake grips. The first makes you appear weak and the second one might give the impression that you are a bully. The ideal handshake involves

facing the other person directly, making firm palm-to-palm contact with the web of your hand (the skin between the thumb and first finger) touching the web of the other person's hand, and matching hand pressure as closely as possible.

Another point to keep in mind is that though body language is universal, it is expressed differently from nation to nation. Nevertheless, the inherent use of it is common to all human beings and is of paramount importance because it is the purest of all human expressions.

Facial Expressions

Your facial features can convey your feelings, mood, attitude, interest, and a whole range of other aspects. When you speak, movements of your eyes, mouth, and facial muscles develop a connection with the listener. Here are some points to keep in mind when it comes to facial features:

1. When speaking to a group of people, try to establish eye contact with all listeners so that everyone feels that you are personally communicating with them.
2. Speaking in an effective and modulated voice according to the intensity of expressions will make communication more powerful.
3. Talking with a smiling face will help you develop a bond as it reflects affability and truthfulness.
4. A good body posture would help you to better manage your voice. Balance your body weight equally on both feet when speaking. A perfectly

balanced body should move harmoniously with the voice.

5. Practise your facial expressions by standing in front of a full-sized mirror and making different facial expressions. It will help you to know which facial expression is appropriate for a particular emotion and how to use it while conversing with others.

Posture

Body posture conveys a wide range of attitudes and is an important aspect of communication because it enhances or contradicts the force of expressions. A positive and correct posture will show that you are deeply enjoying what you are saying. You can add more weight to what you are saying by effectively using your posture which includes moving forward in your seat or bending towards the audience to make a point.

Also, while listening, Leaning forward will indicate that you are interested in the conversation and carefully listening. Leaning back will give the opposite impression. Standing or sitting in a straight posture will give a confident and alert look and set a positive impression. On the other hand, poor posture, a bad posture such as slouching will reflect poor self-image and negative feelings. Hunched back and slumped shoulders will show a lazy, listless, and negligent personality.

Learning and Imbibing Good Posture

Normally, your body will be in the correct posture when it is aligned in the following way: The back is straight, the shoulders are squared and relaxed, the chin is up, the chest is out, and the stomach is tucked in. This will distribute the force of gravity throughout the body and no part of the body will be overstressed.

You can talk to a physiotherapist and get their expert opinion on correct postures for sitting, standing, walking, reading, sleeping, etc. Yoga, sports, and certain games, particularly balancing games, are also good for learning and improving posture. And once you have learnt the correct postures, you will need to keep it in check initially until it becomes a habit.

Another point to note is that your working environment should discourage slouching or any other kind of bad posture. Have your desk at elbow height and never work at a desk that makes you slouch. You also should not work sitting on a couch or lying in the bed. When working on computers and laptops, keep your shoulders back and your back straight as well as keep the bottom of your palms lifted above the keyboard rather than resting on it.

Also, always select furniture that encourages good posture. If you feel uncomfortable while working, change the furniture and make sure that chair mattresses are firm because soft mattress leads to slouching which, in turn, causes discomfort to your back.

Effective Speaking

The voice of a person exposes as much about his personal profile as his appearance. And in today's world, the voice of a person is one of the most important character traits because speaking well translates to effective communication. The skill of putting words together in a meaningful way to reflect thoughts, opinions, and feelings gives several advantages. Well-developed speaking skills will increase your confidence level, greatly enhance your negotiation skills, and enable you to inform, motivate, and guide clearly and confidently. In Gerald Gillis's novel, *Dare Not Blink,* the main character, Dave Paige, manages to move up the corporate ladder mainly because of his skill to present his ideas clearly and convincingly.

Aspects of Effective Speaking

Effective speaking is being able to speak with confidence and clarity, whilst exposing own personality. It comprises four aspects: accent, an effective voice, the effect of breathing on voice and speech, and vocal production. Let's look at these aspects in detail.

I. Accent

Your accent is the way you pronounce different words, vowels, and consonants. Every person has his own accent because of regional and family factors and a different or typical accent is not a speech or language defect. However, an accent becomes a problem if you have difficulty communicating because others are not able to understand what you are trying to say. So, it is important to have an accent that others can understand easily.

Improving Accent

The most internationally-accepted accent today is called the neutral accent which is primarily used to speak English in a universally accepted style. It avoids mother-tongue influence and regional accent. Further, it ensures a clear mode of communication. Therefore, with proper practice and determination, you can modify your accent to communicate more effectively and clearly. Here are a few steps to improve your accent and pronunciation:

1. **Open lips and move**
   Many people, when speaking, normally do not move their lips enough. You should know that the lips position when speaking English is quite different to the lips position when speaking in your mother tongue. This is because English has many open sounds like 'ou' in phone, 'a' in start, 'a' in hat, etc. Thus, you need to practice these open sounds and move your lips to make these sounds clearly and correctly. So, learning to correctly move your lips, especially when speaking English, is quite important. If you are not moving and opening your lips enough, your voice will not be clear as you would only be mumbling. If you can afford to avail training from a conversation expert then that is a great option.

2. **Slow down and speak**
   English is not the first language for most of us and therefore, we pronounce many English words incorrectly and use different stress and rhythms. This gives an improper accent and makes your English difficult to understand. Speaking slowly allows people to understand you as it gives them time to connect to and classify what you are saying. You can

control the speed of your speech by giving more pauses, especially between phrases and sentences. Emphasise the keywords in the message. You can use gestures to emphasise important words. You can also improve by becoming aware of how your lips move. A great way to do this is by recording yourself and then carefully observing how you sound.

3. **Listen more carefully**
   Listen to people who are good at speaking English and observe how they are speaking instead of just paying attention to what they are saying. Take notice of the rhythmic patterns in their speech and the way the pitch of their voice goes up and down. English is a lively language and the rise and fall of voice when talking actually makes the speech clear and easy for others to understand.

4. **Practise pronunciation**
   Many people are unable to change their speech and accent and they continue to have a very heavy accent. Therefore, it is essential to focus specifically on particular areas of pronunciation and try to change sounds and speech patterns. So, for five-to-ten minutes a day, focus on the way people move their lips and the sounds they make. Compare it with the way you move your lips and the sounds you make.

II. An Effective Voice

Voice, like fingerprints and DNA, is an integral component of your identity. The pitch, intonation, and volume of your voice contain the emotional content of your message and express perceptive changes in your intent and mood. An important point to note here is that each person has a somewhat unique voice as the shape and size of the vocal mechanism of every person is different, giving a unique timbre to the voice.

Most people are not aware that their voice plays a crucial role when it comes to achieving success. In fact, the sound of your voice strongly influences how you are viewed in the workplace and the wider society. Communication analytics are of the view that the sound and tone of a person's voice are twice as important as the content.

How to Improve Voice Quality?

As discussed earlier, every organisation likes a person who can speak convincingly and effectively. And whether in the government or private sector, those who are able to give effective presentations are preferred and promoted fast. So, it is important to become a person who can communicate effectively. However, the quality of voice is often overlooked and this can lead to disastrous results. For example, if a person with a soft or phoney voice, it can make their speech seem unpleasant and undermine their message entirely. Therefore, it is important to improve the quality, tone, and expression of your voice through regular practise.

Given below are some suggestions to help you develop a good voice:

1. **Slow down**

   An effective way to improve the clarity of your message is to speak at an understandable speed. Hence, speaking at an optimal pace will allow the audience to understand you better. It will also make you sound more confident and in control. A good benchmark for this is to speak at a pace at which if you were telling a phone number, the person listening should be able to write it down. You can practise the speed of your speech by narrating a long number and writing it in the air.

2. **Breathe**

   If you do not breathe deeply into your chest and abdomen, your voice will sound weaker and shaky. It is not easy to breathe deeply when you are tense or stressed but you should learn to take full-relaxed breaths to deepen your voice in every kind of situation. This will help capture the audience's attention and make you sound more confident.

3. **Watch your posture**

   The way you sit or stand affects the quality of your voice. Your voice will be less effective if your shoulders are tight and hunched up towards your head. Standing or sitting straight will allow you to breathe normally, giving your voice a greater force and clarity. Also, lifting up your chin and tilting your head a little will make your voice sound clearer.

4. **Hydrate**

   Keeping yourself well-hydrated is vital because it improves the quality of your voice. Your vocal cords need to be energetic and vibrating for which your body should have sufficient moisture. And considering that the average vibration rate of the vocal cords for women is 200 times per second and for men, it's about 120 times per second, you can see why your vocal cords require regular lubrication in the form of hydration.

5. **Watch your pitch**

   High-pitched voice gives the impression that you are insecure or nervous. Using the right vocal pitch helps to be a more effective communicator. You can find your perfect pitch by saying 'uh-huh' as if you were casually saying 'yes' to a question. The pitch of your voice when you speak should match the 'uh.'

6. **Avoid yelling**

   Never speak at the top of your voice because it is not good for your vocal cords. Yelling also causes swelling of your vocal cords and strains them, making it difficult for you to speak.

Conclusion

The significance of effective communication skills in both personal and professional spheres cannot be overstated. Throughout this chapter, we have navigated the intricate landscape of communication, uncovering its multi-dimensional nature and far-reaching impact. We have delved into the art of active listening, the power of verbal and nonverbal cues, and the nuances of assertive and empathetic communication.

What emerges as a resounding truth is that communication is the lifeblood of human interaction. It is the bridge that connects us, the tool that resolves conflicts, and the vehicle that conveys our ideas and emotions. In the context of the professional world, strong communication skill is the linchpin of effective leadership, collaboration, and career advancement.

As we move forward, it is essential to recognise that communication skill is not static but continuously evolving. It requires cultivation, refinement, and adaptability to stay relevant in an increasingly interconnected and digital age. The journey to becoming an exceptional communicator is a commitment to self-improvement, an embrace of feedback, and an exploration of new avenues and technologies.

Chapter Four

Thought Leader

Henry Ford is one of the greatest thought leaders in corporate history. In 1891, Ford was working as chief engineer with the Edison Illuminating Company in Detroit and was fascinated by gasoline-powered automobiles. In his spare time, he began working on 'Quadricycle' and developed a simple machine by placing two bicycles side by side and fitting a petrol engine. He worked on the Quadricycle for many years and when it was functioning, he took a Detroit lumber tycoon William H. Murphy for a ride in his hand-built automobile. So fascinated was Murphy by the car that by the time the ride was over, he asked Ford to become his business partner.

The Detroit Automobile Company was set up in 1899 with Ford as superintendent of production. However, the venture only lasted a year because Ford could not produce a car. Undaunted, Ford set up a shop in a converted wagon factory, hired workers, and designed and produced the Model A. Then in 1903, when Ford was forty years old, he founded the Ford Motor Company. At that time, cars were driven by horses and horseless carriages were so expensive that only a few wealthy persons could afford them.

At that time, most other automakers were building luxury cars for the wealthy. But Ford's dream was to produce a car that everyone could afford, and he worked on the Model T which was simpler, more reliable, and cheaper than the Model A. Model T—nicknamed the 'Tin Lizzie'—was officially launched in 1908. The car became extremely popular and did record-breaking sales. But just within a few months, Ford had to stop taking fresh orders as he couldn't keep up with bulging orders.

Ford found a solution to this problem in a 'moving assembly line,' which made his dream a reality. He realised that if a worker did not move from place to place and remained in one assigned place and performed one specific task, more cars could be produced. Ford perfected the system and within a year, the manufacturing time of the car was brought down to just 93 minutes. This also allowed Ford to cut hundreds of dollars off the price of his car and the sales of his cars swelled. With this idea of his, modern mass production was born.

Ford's innovative vision of mass production not only produced the first reliable, affordable automobile for the masses but also triggered a modern industrial revolution and changed not only the US but the whole world.

***

Who Is a Thought Leader?

Thought leaders are opinion makers who inspire others with innovative ideas and turn ideas into reality. They know and show how to overcome industry challenges and are proficient at creating a dedicated team to achieve their desired goals. Some of the most admired thought leaders include Robin Chase, founder of Zipcar, Amanda Nguyen of Rise, and Ron Finley, the co-founder of the charity L.A. Green Grounds who styles himself as the 'Guerrilla Gardener' in order to encourage Angelenos to cultivate vegetable and fruit gardens in vacant lots in deprived neighbourhoods. Leaders like them are changing the world in meaningful ways and motivating others to join their efforts. They create evolutionary and even revolutionary advancements in their fields, influencing others to be open to new ways of thinking.

Fundamentals To Be a Thought Leader

Though the concept of thought leadership was introduced in 1994 by Joel Kurtzman, former editor-in-chief of *Strategy+Business*, today the term has evolved into a more nuanced and multifaceted expression. Let's take a closer look at what goes into making a thought leader.

1. **Visionary**

   A visionary person is someone who has foresight which enables him to look at what's possible in the future. Simply put, a visionary person is innovative, insightful and imaginative. Marcia Wieder, CEO of Dream University and a personal transformation expert, believes that 'a visionary has a big dream, articulates it with clarity so people get it, and expresses it with passion so others can feel it and get excited with them. Most importantly a true visionary has mastered the skill to inspire, invite and enrol others.'

   Visionary leadership is not a new phenomenon in business. Behind the most well-known and most successful businesses, there is the presence of visionary business leaders like Dhirubhai Ambani, Henry Ford, Warren Buffet, Sunil Mittal, Steve

Jobs, Bill Gates, Larry Page, Elon Musk, Michael Dell, and Mark Zuckerberg. The truth is that visionary leadership is needed for the success of a company.

2. **Strategic Thinker**

   A thought leader needs to be adept at creating new ideas and strategies to move towards the goal. This means that he should be able to identify new opportunities for the company and accordingly strategise a steadfast plan.

   Strategic thinking is the skill of thinking to achieve your goals by making effective decisions and developing realistic action plans after analysing critical factors and variables. Thinking strategically is essential for success as it enables you to set clear goals, draw realistic plans, and capitalise on new opportunities. It also allows you to make substantial contributions to you to be successful at your workplace.

3. **Resilient**

   If you want to reach the top and stay there, you should learn how to successfully navigate your way through tough times. Nationwide and Vodafone sponsored a study to find out the relationship between resilience and success and almost all participants who took part in the study said that resilience was an important factor when it came to success.

   There are also multiple advantages to being resilient. It makes you more tactful to weather unexpected challenges as well as more immune against negative emotions and thoughts which, in turn, enable you to deal with issues calmly and logically.

4. **Change Agent**

   Change is an essential part of all businesses and industries. Thus, it is important to move with time and adjust the company's operations in response to increased competition, technological advances, stakeholder expectations, and other pressures. And this is only possible if there is a change agent, a person who promotes and enables progress in the organisation. This process entails promoting the use of new technology and innovations, adopting a new management structure, and transforming old business models into new ones.

   Being open to change has become extremely important in today's business environment because if the organisation does not change in the fast-developing corporate world, it would soon stagnate and miss new opportunities.

Conclusion

The concept of a thought leader transcends mere innovation and expertise; it embodies a profound commitment to shaping the future. Thought leaders are not content with the status quo; they are visionaries who constantly challenge norms, inspire change, and ignite conversations that push society forward. In today's rapidly evolving world, the role of thought leaders is more crucial than ever. They serve as beacons of inspiration, guiding us through the turbulent waters of uncertainty and complexity.

As we have explored in this chapter, thought leadership is not confined to a select few. Anyone with a passion, knowledge, and a platform can become a thought leader, making it a democratic and inclusive force for progress. Thought leaders harness the power of their unique perspectives, compelling narratives, and unwavering dedication to effect meaningful change. Furthermore, the impact of thought leaders extends far beyond individual success. Their ideas have the potential to transform industries, spark social movements, and redefine the way we perceive the world. Thus, it is imperative that we recognise the importance of nurturing thought leadership in our communities, organizations, and personal endeavours. By understanding the essence of thought leadership, we can unlock our own potential to lead, inspire, and contribute to a brighter future. In a world hungering for innovation and progress, thought leaders are the catalysts for change, and their influence will continue to shape our destiny for generations to come.

Chapter Five

Creativity

Two nine-year-old students, Shweta and Rani, won the second prize for direction in the Little Directors category at the 18th International Children's Film Festival in Hyderabad in 2013. The astonishing fact in this case was the backstory of the girls. Both girls came from unprivileged backgrounds—Rani's parents were daily labourers and Shweta's father worked as a security guard— and were students of a non-discrepant municipal school in New Chaukhandi, a village three kilometres away from Rajouri Garden in West Delhi. And though both were deprived of basic facilities, they had dreams and a desire to do something innovative.

Their film, *Phoolwati Amma*, which was based on the real-life story of a school sweeper, was picked up out of 600 entries from across the world. The film starts with a shot of Phoolwati at work, followed by an interview about her days at the school, and ends with school children giving her gifts at her farewell after her retirement.

When I read the story in The Times of India newspaper on December 4, 2013, it made me realise the immense power of creativity over technical and knowledge-based skills. But I wasn't the first one to make this observation. Even Einstein had said, 'Imagination is more important than knowledge.'

In this chapter, we will explore the importance of developing creativity and how we can do so.

***

Importance of Creativity in Business

Creativity is the ability to perceive the world in new ways and bring something new into existence. In the last century, creativity and innovation have become highly sought-after skills for achieving success in business, administration, and management because all problems require creative problem-solving. Creativity and innovation are closely associated because innovation is not possible without creativity. While creativity is the ability to generate new and inimitable ideas, innovation is what makes creativity possible.

In today's highly competitive world, every corporate entity wants to work on unique ideas stimulated by creativity and innovation. That's why top management looks for new ideas in production, processing, marketing, and financial management. An NYSE:IBM survey of more than 1,500 CEOs from 60 countries and 33 industries stated that more than rigour, management, discipline, integrity, or even vision, creativity was essential for success in an increasingly complex world.

Since every industry is facing new challenges, major MNCs, like Apple, are making serious efforts to face the challenge by introducing new ideas. Companies have found that customers just do not come to buy their products but more for the environment in the shop. For example, Starbucks, a global coffee company with over 23,000 storefronts selling coffee and espresso drinks in 75 countries, realised that customers come to their coffee shop just not to drink coffee but more for the ambience—which includes warmth shown by the workers, welcoming interior colour scheme, good music, and often, furniture or art—than for the coffee being sold. Barista, a coffee outlet, is another example where you can sit for hours reading newspapers and magazines, work on your laptop, read your own book, or play musical instruments that are available there.

A brand like Apple also realises the need for creativity in developing its brand and market. Apple's stores are clean and modern which encourage its managers to think creatively and differently, and this step helped to make Apple number one in the Boston Consulting Group's list of 'The Most Innovative Companies' for 11 years in a row. Apple understood that creativity is essential in business because it's a differentiator. If you compare an iPhone with a Samsung handset, both may look very similar. But once you start using it, you will find more creative features and aspects in an iPhone.

Elements of Creativity

In simple terms, creativity can be defined as a passion to do things in a different way and develop new and unique ideas. Out-of-the-box thinking is essential for creativity to reach innovative solutions. Let's explore some core elements of creativity.

1. **Readiness to do something new**

   You can be creative only when you are willing to do something different. A creative person pushes himself to go where no one has gone before and do things that no one has done before. This makes creative people also visionary in a way as they are able to envision something which is not there in the world.

2. **Accept challenges**

   The second element is to accept challenges, which means that a creative person is not afraid to take risks. When you accept a new challenge, you get an opportunity for growth and a likelihood of developing a new skill. This also makes you more valuable to your organisation. Accepting challenges gives you the exhilaration of victory,' believed the Second World War veteran, General George S. Patton.

3. **Be open to criticism**

   No one likes to be criticised but constructive criticism is always good because it allows you to learn and grow. Thus, criticism helps in realising how you can improve your work and also gives you a new angle to think. When you are working on a problem and are not able to find solutions, inviting criticism would provide you feedback that, in turn, can show you the way forward. Simply put, criticism should be encouraged as it would give you a new perspective and indicate points that you may have overlooked.

Promoting Creativity

Often, creativity is considered to be an innate quality but new studies have shown that this skill can be developed. Here are a few ways that will help you boost your creativity quotient:

1. **Recognising Patterns**

This is a process by which you use multiple rationalities to make decisions. While working on a problem, your brain develops certain patterns that help you in identifying certain objects and situations. For example, we know that large, upright, flat, and rectangular pieces of wood are doors which can be opened and closed to pass through different rooms. Therefore, you will surely recognise a door and know how to use it even when you come across a door you have never seen before. Without this ability, we would not be able to do even the simplest tasks.

Nobel Laureate Herbert Simon believed that pattern recognition to be the strongest aspect of the decision-making process. Not only that, but patterns are also an integral part of nature because they can be found everywhere, in science, sports, games, music, etc. Therefore, strong pattern recognition skill is important as it prepares the mind to be more active and powerful.

Simply stated, pattern recognition is the process of training ourselves to spot trends. And by becoming better at it, you can sort out objects and situations in your mind and determine the next steps you should take. For example, while driving, you use pattern recognition because you know about the traffic patterns. You know that at a four-street crossing, yellow lights will always turn red and, therefore, even if you are driving on a new road, you will be able to safely navigate by your knowledge of traffic patterns. There are many activities as well that can help improve your pattern recognition abilities. Chess is a great game that requires thinking strategically, weighing available options, and making strategic decisions, leading to better cognitive and problem-solving skills. It has been proved that chess players outperform others in the areas of fluency, originality, and flexibility. It is no wonder that thirty countries of the world have selected chess as a tool for teaching students better thinking skills, strategic planning, and decision-making.

2. **Developing Divergent and Convergent Thinking**

Convergent and divergent are totally opposite to each other in many ways but both are extremely important for promoting creativity. Convergent thinking is the process of figuring out a concrete solution to any problem whereas divergent thinking is the process of imagining several possible solutions to generate creative ideas. In other words, convergent thinking is a straightforward process that focuses on figuring out the most effective solution to a problem, whereas divergent thinking requires opening the mind in various ways to find multiple solutions to a problem. The characteristics of convergent thinking include speed, accuracy, and logic, while the features of divergent thinking include spontaneity and a non-linear mindset.

Though completely different, both thinking processes can be employed to explore creativity. Divergent thinking empowers the person to think outside-the-box to find new and innovative solutions. Convergent thinking's vital role is to make sure that necessary standards and protocols are followed while trying to find solutions. Intelligent thinkers use both strategies to generate original and credible ideas.

3. **Provide an Environment Congenial to Creativity**

The right working environment is essential for developing creativity. Though creativity emerges in the brain, many psychologists and neuroscientists believe that many unintended factors in your physical environment significantly influence the creative output of a person. Kurt Lewin, a German-born, American social psychologist, believed that human behaviour was a function of both the person as well as the physical environment he/she works in. Therefore, making a physical environment that puts a person at ease and makes him feel relaxed and safe will get the best creativity out of a person.

The working environment can be made more creative-friendly by adopting various methods. First, the lighting in the work area should be as natural as possible because it boosts the immune system and increases dopamine levels which influence many other functions including memory, sleep, mood, behaviour and cognition. It also lowers cortisol levels and brings up superior creativity by inspiring a feeling of freedom. Therefore, if you work in a naturally lit room, you will feel less anxious, happier, and more productive.

Secondly, the noise level should be at a comfortable level. Calm and relaxing sounds can get the creative juices flowing. Thirdly, the temperature in the work area should be soothing to the body and mind. Several studies have found that a constant temperature of 21 degrees Celsius keeps people focused on work. Fourthly, you should use eco-friendly and green materials at your workplace as they act as natural air purifiers and also release plenty of oxygen. Also, greenery has a calming effect and therefore, makes it easier for you to enter your flow state.

Conclusion

All in all, the significance of creativity in all aspects of life can never be overstated. I would conclude this chapter with an enchanting fable from Hindu mythology that highlights the ingenious use of creativity.

Lord Shiva and Parvati had two sons, Ganesha and Kartikeya, whom they loved dearly. One day, *devas* (divine beings) gave one divine fruit to Shiva and Parvati and told them that it was a special fruit and anyone who ate it will get the supreme knowledge and would become eternal. Knowing the fruit's significance, both the sons wanted to eat it and it developed into a squabble between them. Shiva came out with a solution and told the two sons that the son who would circle the world three times and come back first will get the fruit.

Kartikeya, who rode a peacock, took this challenge seriously and straightaway began to circle the world. But Ganesha, the god of wisdom, was fully aware that he couldn't defeat Kartikeya in this race because of his huge belly and his vehicle, which was a slow-moving mouse.

But Ganesha used his wisdom and started circling his parents and did it three times. Shiva and Parvati were amused and wanted to know what he was doing.

Ganesha replied that his parents were his whole world and so, he was circling the world. Both Shiva and Parvati were pleased to listen to the argument of Ganesha and gave him the divine fruit.

Chapter Six

Mind-Management

Our brain and mind together act as a computer. They control everything and have all the necessary connections, storage, memory, and processing power you need to function as a human being. Moreover, we can say that the brain is the hardware, and the mind is the software, collecting, storing, and managing all information. In fact, your mind manages all your thinking, creativity, and behaviours which play a crucial role in your life. Not only that, but the mind also has limitless potential and can open doors to new and exciting worlds and enable you to charter new territories and achieve the impossible. Thus, effective and efficient use of our mind can help us succeed in the highly competitive world and this skill is termed mind-management skills. Let's explore this aspect in detail.

What Is Mind Management?

Simply put, mind management consists of reprogramming your mind to create the right mindset, which, in turn, will enable you to achieve your goals and aspirations. In other words, it is the skill of controlling, organising, and coordinating the activities of your mind so that you can make decisions to achieve definite objectives.

The reason we require mind-management skills is because our mind is a thinking engine which keeps on pumping out thoughts (an average person has about 7,000 thoughts every day), and through mind management, we can deliberately and consciously control our mind and the direction of our thoughts to create conditions that benefit us and develop our full potential. This technique gives us the power to focus our mind on what is really important.

But only a small number of people have the capability to focus their mind. However, with proper training and practice, we too can learn this skill and gain control over our thinking process and attain a high level of insight.

The Importance of Mind Management in Business

In the fast-paced and highly competitive world of business, technical expertise and knowledge are essential, but they are no longer sufficient on their own. Success in modern business demands mind-management skills. This skill encompasses a range of psychological and emotional abilities that enable individuals to navigate the challenges of the business world with resilience, adaptability, and a clear, focused mindset. In this section, we will delve into the significance of mind-management skills in business and why they are crucial for achieving sustainable success.

1. **Enhancing Productivity**

   One of the primary benefits of effective mind management is improved productivity. When individuals can manage their mind effectively, they are better equipped to concentrate on tasks, make sound decisions, and execute projects efficiently.

This, in turn, contributes to higher productivity and better overall performance.

2. **Reducing Burnout**

   In business, burnout is a prevalent issue, and it can have severe consequences for both employees and organisations. Mind-management skills help individuals recognise the signs of burnout and implement strategies to prevent it. Techniques such as mindfulness meditation, time management, and self-care practices enable individuals to recharge and maintain their energy levels, reducing the risk of burnout.

3. **Enhancing Resilience**

   Business is full of uncertainties, and setbacks are common. Mind-management skills cultivate resilience—the ability to bounce back from challenges and setbacks. Resilient individuals view failures as opportunities for growth rather than insurmountable obstacles. This mindset fosters a culture of innovation and adaptability within an organisation.

4. **Strategic Decision-Making**

   In today's complex business environment, decision-making is rarely straightforward. Successful businesses require leaders and teams who can make strategic decisions that align with the organization's goals and values. Leaders with strong mind-management skill are more adept at making sound and holistic decisions that take into account a wide range of factors. This leads to decisions that are not only fruitful but also effective and efficient.

5. **Embracing Change**

   Mind-management skill helps individuals embrace change rather than fear it. They can adjust their mindset to see change as an opportunity for growth and learning rather than a threat to stability. This adaptability is vital for staying competitive in rapidly changing industries.

6. **Promoting Innovation**

   Innovation is the lifeblood of business growth. Mind-management skill fosters a creative mindset that encourages individuals to think outside the box, generate fresh ideas, and take calculated risks. Innovative solutions often lead to a competitive edge and market leadership.

7. **Clarity of Thought**

   Mind-management skill contribute to clarity of thought, helping individuals cut through complexity to identify the core issues and make informed decisions. This mental clarity is essential for setting strategic directions and goals.

8. **Risk Management**

   A business inherently involves risk. Mind-management skill enables individuals to assess risks objectively and make calculated decisions. This balanced approach to risk management can prevent catastrophic failures and protect the organization's reputation.

9. **Self-Care**

   Mind-management skills emphasise self-care and well-being. Individuals who prioritise their mental and physical health are better equipped to handle the demands of the business world while maintaining a healthy work-life balance.

10. **Sustainable Success**

    Sustainable success in business is not just about achieving short-term goals; it's about maintaining performance and well-being over the long term. Mind-management skill provides the foundation for this sustainability by fostering resilience, adaptability, and a balanced approach to work and life.

    In the competitive and ever-changing landscape of business, mind-management skills have become a non-negotiable asset. They empower individuals and organisations to thrive, innovate, and adapt to challenges effectively. By focusing on various facets of mind management, you can unlock your full potential and achieve sustainable success in a rapidly evolving world.

    As businesses continue to evolve and globalise, the cultivation of mind-management skills will remain an essential strategy for staying ahead of the curve and making a lasting impact in the world of commerce.

How to Develop Mind-Management Skills

Managing your mind is an integral part of attaining success in life. If you do not manage your mind, you would be directionless and would be rudderless in life's sea, drifting about without attaining your targets. But if you want to get what you want, develop a friendship with your mind so that it works for you and not against you.

In this section, we will explore various ways to develop and enhance this essential skill to foster personal growth and achieve a balanced, fulfilling life.

1. **Mindfulness Meditation**

   Mindfulness is a powerful practice that involves paying deliberate attention to the present moment without judgment. It is a cornerstone of mind management, as it helps individuals become more aware of their thoughts, emotions, and reactions. Developing mindfulness can be achieved through mindfulness meditation.

   How to Practice Mindfulness Meditation

   - Find a Quiet Space: Choose a quiet place where you won't be disturbed.
   - Assume a Comfortable Posture: Sit or lie down in a comfortable position. You can use a cushion or chair for added comfort.
   - Focus on Your Breath: Close your eyes and focus your attention on your breath. Pay attention to the sensation of the breath entering and leaving your nostrils or the rise and fall of your abdomen.

- Let Thoughts Come and Go: As thoughts arise, acknowledge them without judgment and gently return your focus to your breath.
- Start with Short Sessions: Begin with 5-10 minutes of meditation and gradually extend the duration as you become more comfortable.
- Practice Regularly: Consistency is key. Aim to practice mindfulness meditation daily to reap its benefits.

Benefits of Mindfulness Meditation

- Stress Reduction: Mindfulness meditation is proven to reduce stress and promote relaxation.
- Improved Focus: It enhances concentration and cognitive function.
- Emotional Regulation: It helps manage emotions and reduce reactivity.
- Enhanced Self-Awareness: Mindfulness cultivates a deeper understanding of one's thoughts and feelings.

2. **Cognitive Behavioural Therapy (CBT)**

Cognitive Behavioural Therapy is a therapeutic approach that helps individuals recognise and change negative thought patterns and behaviours. It is particularly effective for managing stress, anxiety, and depression.

How to Practice CBT Techniques

- Identify Negative Thoughts: Pay attention to your thought patterns and identify negative or irrational thoughts.

- Challenge Negative Thoughts: Question the validity of negative thoughts. Are they based on evidence? Are they exaggerated?
- Replace Negative Thoughts: Replace negative thoughts with more balanced and positive ones.
- Behavioural Changes: Identify behaviours that reinforce negative thinking and work on changing them.
- Practice Relaxation Techniques: Incorporate relaxation techniques, such as deep breathing or progressive muscle relaxation, to manage stress.

Benefits of CBT

- Improved Mental Health: CBT is highly effective in managing anxiety and depression.
- Enhanced Problem-Solving: It promotes more rational and constructive problem-solving.
- Stress Reduction: CBT helps individuals manage stress and cope with challenging situations.

3. **Resilience Training**

Resilience is the ability to bounce back from adversity and maintain mental and emotional well-being. Resilience training helps individuals develop the capacity to adapt and thrive in the face of challenges.

How to Build Resilience

- Develop a Growth Mindset: Embrace challenges as opportunities for growth and learning.
- Build a Support Network: Cultivate strong relationships with friends, family, and mentors who can provide emotional support.
- Self-Care: Prioritise self-care practices, including exercise, healthy eating, and sufficient sleep.
- Problem-Solving Skills: Enhance your problem-solving skills to effectively address challenges.
- Emotional Regulation: Practice emotional regulation techniques to manage stress and anxiety.

Benefits of Resilience Training

- Improved Mental Health: Resilience training can reduce symptoms of anxiety and depression.
- Enhanced Adaptability: It helps individuals navigate change and uncertainty with confidence.
- Increased Satisfaction: Resilient individuals often report higher life satisfaction.

4. **Continuous Learning and Growth**

   The development of mind-management skills is an ongoing process. It involves a commitment to continuous learning and personal growth.

Ways to Foster Continuous Learning

- Read Widely: Explore books and articles on psychology, self-help, and personal development.
- Take Courses: Enrol in workshops or online courses that focus on mind management and emotional intelligence.
- Seek Feedback: Ask for feedback from peers, mentors, or coaches to identify areas for improvement.
- Set Personal Goals: Establish clear and measurable goals for enhancing mind-management skills.
- Practice Self-Reflection: Regularly reflect on your experiences, emotions, and reactions to gain self-awareness.

Benefits of Continuous Learning

- Enhanced Adaptability: Continuously learning new skills makes it easier to adapt to changing circumstances.
- Personal Growth: Learning fosters personal growth and development.
- Improved Problem-Solving: Continuous learning can provide you with new tools and perspectives for solving problems.

5. **Professional Coaching and Therapy**

   Sometimes, developing mind-management skills may require professional guidance. Coaches and therapists can offer valuable insights and strategies for personalised guidance, support, and strategies tailored to an individual's unique needs and goals.

Types of Professional Coaching

i. **Executive Coaching:** For business leaders and professionals, executive coaches offer specialized guidance in areas such as leadership, emotional intelligence, and stress management. They help individuals identify strengths and areas for improvement, set goals, and implement strategies for personal and career growth.

ii. **Life Coaching:** Life coaches assist individuals in various aspects of life, including personal development, goal setting, and work-life balance. They help clients gain clarity about their values, priorities, and aspirations, fostering holistic personal growth.

iii. **Career Coaching:** Career coaches focus on helping individuals make informed career choices, navigate career transitions, and develop skills for success in the workplace. They offer support in resume building, interview preparation, and career planning.

Conclusion

Developing mind-management skills is an ongoing journey that requires commitment, self-awareness, and a variety of strategies and resources. Whether through mindfulness meditation, cognitive-behavioural therapy, resilience building, continuous learning, or professional coaching and therapy, individuals have a wealth of tools at their disposal to cultivate this essential skill.

Investing in the development of mind-management skills not only enhances one's personal well-being but also contributes to success in various facets of life, including career, relationships, and overall satisfaction. By choosing the approaches that resonate most with their needs and goals, you can embark on a path of personal growth and resilience, ultimately unlocking your full potential.

Chapter Seven

Critical Thinking

One stormy night, a man was lost in the forest and with nowhere to go, he reached the door of a monastery. He shouted for someone to open the door, but no one responded. Finally, he saw a stone and hit the door with it. A monk came out and took him to a room that had a sleeping mat. Tired, but consoled, he put the stone on the floor and fell into sound sleep.

The next morning, when he got up, he tried to open the door of his room to ask for food, but the door was locked. He shouted, but no one answered again. At last, he picked up the stone and pounded on the door. A monk soon appeared and led him into another room that had food, water, and a pallet. The traveller bathed, ate, and rested.

Afterwards, he wanted to leave but found the door locked again. So, when he pounded the door with the stone, he was again answered and taken to a more comfortable room.

And so, he lived like that for a number of days, carrying his heavy stone from room to room, and using it to open each succeeding door. Ultimately, he no longer shouted or tried to open the door, but immediately pounded the door with his stone when he wanted to leave.

One day, when he was pounding heavily on a door, the monk on the other side said to him, 'Why don't you try to open the door yourself?' The man pushed against the door and it opened easily into the next room.

The monk said, 'Is it always necessary to carry your heavy stone and beat upon the door? There are many that are not locked.'

The moral of the story is that success lies in properly and holistically thinking about the problem at hand and tackling it in the right way.

* * *

Thinking is an unbelievable activity, and we seldom realise its importance because we mechanically indulge in it all the time. Research has proved that we never stop thinking; ideas keep flowing inside our mind. This can be seen from the fact that we speak 140 to 180 words per minute, but we think 1300 to 1800 words per minute. This phenomenon explains why our mind sometimes wanders when we are listening to someone or when we are speaking.

But a common misconception is that everyone thinks the same way and that thinking is not a big deal as everyone can do it. The truth is that thinking is a skill which can be developed in order to better analyse and evaluate a situation or an issue and accordingly form a judgment. This is known as critical thinking, and it can help you achieve success in all professions.

All industries also realise the importance of critical thinking and thereby, select persons with good thinking skills. Many of the highest-paying jobs are given to those who can critically think. In job interviews, questions are asked to test critical thinking and it is also a deciding factor at the time of promotion.

But before we look into ways we can develop our critical thinking skills, let's see what differentiates critical thinking from normative thinking.

Thinking Versus Critical Thinking

Thinking is the mental process that enables you to form opinions, without critical reasoning, about people, things, places, etc. Critical thinking is more than just thinking as it also involves 'thinking about thinking'. It is a deeper form of thinking about a specific issue or situation before actually taking a decision and going into action. Thus, critical thinking is a longer process and takes time as your mind considers all issues, suppositions, and varying aspects and asks questions pertaining to why, who, what, where, and when in a particular situation before forming an opinion.

If you are a critical thinker, you will be open-minded and know what other possibilities are and thus, not jump to conclusions. You would conduct thorough research before you formulate reasonable arguments. Critical thinking is an ongoing process and is learnt through active practise and constant use.

Hence, we can see how critical thinking is different from regular thinking as it is more reflective and independent than ordinary thinking. It requires employing strategies like theorising, evaluating, homogenising, and appraising information gathered during the critical thinking process.

Benefits of Critical Thinking

The concept of critical thinking goes way back. During the Hellenistic period, the Socratic method (named after the Greek philosopher Socrates) can be shown to have elements of what we today refer to as critical thinking. Centuries later, Roman Emperor Marcus Aurelius Antoninus, who was also a stoic philosopher, warned in his meditations that 'everything we hear is an opinion, not a fact; everything we see is a perspective, not the truth.' This line has echoes of critical thinking when it comes to seeing the truth or reality. Since then, a galaxy of thinkers, including Galileo, W. E. B. Du Bois, Albert Einstein, Bertrand Russell, Martin Luther King Jr., and many others have lauded the benefits of critical thinking.

So, if this skill has been praised over centuries, there must be true benefits to it. Let's explore them.

1. **Promotes Creativity**

   It is not a coincidence that creative thinkers are also effective critical thinkers because any effort to be creative requires the ability to think critically. We can come up with new and inventive ideas only when we can analyse an issue properly and accordingly fine-tune our solutions. Creative thinkers also raise queries about various aspects related to a problem or a task at hand and try to find out the 'how' or 'why not'. Thus, critical thinking is important when it comes to assessing new ideas, deciding on the best ones and modifying them if necessary. In other words, creativity and innovation are only possible when we have the asset of critical thinking.

2. **Promotes Efficiency**

   Critical thinking enables you to become more efficient as it allows you to consider all options before making a decision. This, in turn, provides you with the most practical and efficient ways of achieving a goal. Simply put, critical thinkers follow the principle: 'work smarter, not harder'.

3. **Builds Problem-Solving Ability**

   If you possess the skill to think critically, you are a good problem-solver. Albert Einstein once said, 'It's not that I'm so smart; it's just that I stay with problems longer.' So, when he was given an hour to solve a problem, he would spend five minutes on the solution and the other fifty-five minutes defining and researching the problem. Thus, what he implies here is that to really understand a problem you have to have level-headed critical thinking ability and only then you can be an effective problem-solver.

4. **Makes You More Aware**

   Critical thinking makes you realise the difference between a rational thought and an emotional response which is the adversary of reasoning. When you think critically, you understand your own viewpoint and also think through the perspective of others and your conclusion will be based on fact and not emotions.

Pillars of Critical Thinking

The following are important aspects that make up critical thinking:

1. **Observation**

   Observation is the ability to use your senses to understand what is happening around you. This skill is elementary to critical thinking because if you are observant, you can quickly feel and identify a problem when it arises. Also, you can comprehend why something might become a problem and, therefore, can foresee the problem before it happens. Observation skills can be improved by slowing down your speed of managing information and paying closer attention to your surroundings.

2. **Analysis**

   After identifying the problem, you have to analyse it, which requires effective diagnostic skills. The skill of analysing and evaluating a situation requires you to know facts, data, and information about the problems that are important. Apart from gathering unbiased information, this aspect also involves raising relevant questions about the data to ensure that it is accurate, and findings are evaluated objectively. This is an important step as ideal decisions can only be made on sound analysis.

3. **Inference**

   After analysing the problem, a conclusion has to be drawn on the basis of collected data which is known as inference or deduction. This involves correctly interpreting the information gathered and accordingly drawing answers. Inference skills can be developed by focusing on making intelligent deductions and not drawing quick conclusions.

4. **Execution**

   After identifying, analysing, and finding possible solutions, you have to finally execute the solution. It requires implementing the best solution and ensuring that it is working as it was planned.

How to Improve Critical Thinking Skills

Following are the ways to improve your critical thinking skills:

1. **Ask basic questions**

   'Though the world is complicated, it does not mean that every problem requires a complicated solution,' said Stephen J. Dubner, an award-winning author and journalist who co-authored the highly successful *Freakonomics* book series. The thing to understand here is that many times, the original question gets lost because its explanation becomes extremely complex. Therefore, you should go back to the basic or core question when finding a solution to the problem. Following are some basic questions you can raise when thinking about a problem:

   - What are we trying to prove, disprove, establish, and criticise?
   - What is being omitted?
   - What is already known about the problem?

2. **Question your assumptions**

   An assumption is an untested idea and therefore, the conclusions based on assumptions have to be considered critically. Therefore, think carefully about your assumptions because they may not be true. All thinkers, from Newton to Einstein to Yitang Zhang questioned normative assumptions which led them to innovative and counter-intuitive solutions. Einstein questioned the assumption that Newtonian laws of motion could perfectly describe the world. He developed an entirely new framework for looking at the world. Therefore, you should think carefully about your assumptions when analysing and concluding any problem.

3. **Know your mental processes**
   The critical thinking method is only effective when we are able to account for our biases when analysing and finding a solution to a problem. Therefore, a critical thinker needs to be aware of his mental biases and personal prejudices and how they influence their decisions and solutions.

4. **Evaluate failures and mistakes**
   An important way to improve your critical thinking is by taking into account all the previous failures and mistakes. By including them in your purview, you boost the scope of your thinking and make it more resilient as it will consider the previous history and experiences when working on a new problem.

5. **Think through the pros and cons**
   Every problem is not simple and, therefore, every decision cannot be clear-cut. Many times you do

not know which way to go. In such a situation, draw all the pros and cons of each solution. Write down all the advantages and disadvantages without preferring a choice over the others. After drawing the list of pros and cons, decide on the solution keeping in mind that the right decision might not be the one that had the highest set of positives and the least number of negatives. One single advantage or disadvantage can be so strong that it can shift the judgment in its favour. The advantage of considering pros and cons is that you can know what all your opportunities, risks, and consequences are. This would require you to keep your thinking process flexible and open to new facts.

Focused Mind and Critical Thinking

Focus is the foundation of critical thinking and involves the ability to concentrate on the work and avoid all distractions. If you do not have a focused mind, your ability to think will weaken and the quality of the work will be poor because of a digressing mind. Therefore, you can think critically and effectively when your mind is focused.

Let's look at some ways we can improve our focus.

1. **Avoid a cluttered mind**

   You cannot focus with a disordered mind that is occupied with too many things you want to do during the day. You have to train yourself to prioritise the tasks. The less cluttered your mind, the better will be your ability to focus. Research at the Center on Everyday Lives and Families at the University of California at Los Angeles (UCLA) has proved that clutter has a profound effect on self-esteem and mood. A study of thirty-two families showed a link between high cortisol (stress hormone) levels of women who had too many house jobs to do.

2. **Design an organised workspace**

   You should have a clean desk that is not crowded with unnecessary junk like pictures, stationery items, assorted knickknacks, souvenirs, and curios. If your workspace is unorganised and is filled up with assorted castoffs, your mind will get distracted. You will vastly improve your focus if you make your work area less congested by removing unnecessary stuff. A few family photos and mementos can make your desk an inviting place to work and it will not disturb your focus. Remember anything that does not encourage you to work is a distraction.

3. **Avoid unnecessary gadgets**

   Though modern gadgets help us save time in many of our day-to-day tasks, they also distract us from completely focusing on our tasks. Digital gadgets like laptops, tablets, and smartphones are the biggest disturbers when you work because of the endless pings and notifications. Psychologists recommend that the study room should be a gadget-free area.

4. **Get some fresh air**

   When you work for long hours, your mind gets tired which, in turn, hampers your focus. In such situations, taking a quick walk outside can be a good idea as it will increase the blood flow to your brain. The fresh air will refresh you and improve the quality of your work. Some deep breathing and light exercise can also energise your mind and help in sustaining focus.

5. **Play games**

   Games such as Sudoku, chess, and Scrabble are great exercises to improve concentration. Such activities need you to focus your mind to solve them. Even solving puzzles, crosswords, etc., would aid in improving your concentration.

Conclusion

The journey through this chapter on critical thinking has been a voyage of intellectual empowerment. We have armed ourselves with the tools to discern fact from fiction, clarity from confusion, and reason from rhetoric. Critical thinking is not merely a skill; it is a mindset, a way of life that empowers us to question, analyse, and ultimately make more informed decisions.

In an age characterised by the rapid dissemination of information and the proliferation of misinformation, the need for critical thinking has never been more urgent. Moreover, critical thinking extends its influence beyond individual benefit. It fosters collaborative problem-solving, constructive dialogue, and the pursuit of knowledge in its purest form. By embracing the principles of critical thinking, we are not only equipping ourselves to thrive in an ever-changing world but also contributing to a more rational, informed, and enlightened society.

Chapter Eight

Decision-Making and Problem-Solving Skills

Several centuries back, tradesmen travelled in groups to buy and sell goods. They followed a code of conduct and always kept their commitments and honoured their deal. This made them reliable which, in turn, brought them more business.

On one occasion, a group of tradesmen undertook a very profitable deal which consisted of transporting goods from one city to another but there was a challenge—they had to take a new route and cross a long and difficult desert. The traders took a caravan and reached the edge of the desert. Soon, the leader of the group realised that the sand in the desert became so hot during the day that they and their camels could not walk on it. Their problem was exacerbated by the fact that they had no access to water throughout their journey. After considering all the pros and cons, the leader decided to travel at night when the sand cooled down. He also decided to hire a local guide to help them cross the desert without facing any problems.

The traders' group began their journey, with the guide, after stocking sufficient water for the journey. But the journey was so tough that after two nights', everyone was tired and exhausted as they could neither sleep during the day because of extreme heat and bright sunlight nor the night since they were travelling constantly. Therefore, when the caravan began its journey on the third night, most of them, including the guide, dozed off within a few hours.

The unguided camel continued walking and the caravan followed it. The guide abruptly woke up once the night's journey had concluded and noticed that the caravan was back at the starting point. After setting up the camp, the caravan's leader realised that they did not have sufficient water to last them through their journey. Understanding the severity of the situation, the leader began to think of a solution and decided to find out if there was water in the surrounding area. As he was moving around, he found small patches of green grass indicating the presence of water which kept the grass alive despite excessive heat. The traders began to dig and soon found a big hard rock which was difficult to break. All the remaining travellers were not hopeful that they would find water and were frustrated at the leader's decision to break the rock. But the leader remained steadfast and composed throughout this entire ordeal. He had already noticed that the rock was wet which indicated the presence of water beneath it. All of them began to hit the rock with a rod and soon, a strong stream of water gushed out and every traveller was able to quench his thirst and fill their containers with water. They finally arrived at their destination and were able to deliver the goods on time.

***

To progress in the twenty-first-century work culture, decision-making and problem-solving are essential skills to have, especially for entrepreneurial leaders and think-tank experts. And like any other skill, these skills need to be developed and sharpened by practising them so that we are ready to take on the challenges of the world. Also, though decision-making and problem-solving might seem similar, there are subtle differences between them. In this chapter, we will explore both of these skills separately.

What Is Decision-Making?

Decision-making is the process of selecting the best option among the various alternatives. And the art of good decision-making involves evaluating all alternatives, analysing their pros and cons, and then picking the best one. In a way, this is a skill that you would require at every step of your way as you move up in your career. Also, apart from work, making quick and accurate decisions can help you greatly in other dimensions of your life as well. Therefore, it is essential to master the art of decision-making.

Learning Decision-Making

As discussed, decision-making is an important skill to develop if you want to be successful in life. The process of learning decision-making skills should start early in life and as you grow, you should take more and more decisions and learn from the successes you achieve and the mistakes you make. The important point to remember here is that you will be unable to make independent decisions if you let others make decisions for you.

Now let's look at a four-step strategy for decision-making.

Four-Step Strategy for Decision-Making

1. **Identify the problem**

   Before you start with any plan of action for an issue at hand, you need to properly identify the issue and the challenges it poses. If working in a group, problems should be discussed by the team so that there is complete agreement. The group leader should write down the problem accurately before discussing it.

2. **Consider possible options**

   The next step is to discuss various solutions to the problem. Brainstorming is the best way to consider various suggestions and weigh out their effectiveness. All suggested options should be written down, no matter how silly or insignificant they might seem. When no more ideas are coming, cross out the weaker ideas so that the minimum number of possible solutions remain out of which one is to be selected.

3. **Evaluate each option and select the best**

   The shortlisted options should be evaluated thoroughly. Each option should be discussed, and its various aspects should be considered in detail.

4. **Make an action plan**

   Once the final decision has been taken, the next step is to prepare an action plan for implementing the decision. The success or failure of the solution also depends on how good the implementation plan is. The formula for making a good action plan is to envisage the step-by-step working of the solution and foresee what can go wrong.

What Is Problem-Solving?

Problem-solving specifically relates to finding the best solution to an issue. The ability to solve problems quickly and accurately provides a number of unique benefits apart from boosting your career. It gives you confidence and courage, enhances your self-image and self-esteem, and also creates a dynamic personality that is full of energy and vigour. Basically, if you learn to solve problems effectively and efficiently, you will be able to succeed in your life throughout.

But the truth is that everyone does not possess good problem-solving skills. In fact, most wait for their seniors to guide them and solve the problems at hand. But, if you want to be successful, you must possess the ability to solve problems on your own. You are supposed to solve them independently and therefore, you should learn problem-solving methods and techniques before you join any profession.

Learning Problem-Solving

You can learn creative problem-solving skills and techniques by working with experienced people. Also, referring to various case studies relating to a specific problem is a great way to improve your problem-solving skills.

Whatever may be the level of your problem-solving skill, you can always improve it by developing the right mindset. The following pointers will help you become a better problem-solver:

1. **Don't focus on the problem but on the solution**
   Neurologists believe that your brain will find it difficult if you focus only on the problem. They say that you should always tell your brain to find solutions and keep on thinking about the possible causes of the problem. A positive approach is to acknowledge the problem and then switch to seeking possible solutions.

2. **Ensure that you are solving the right problem**
   Properly evaluating the problem at hand is an essential part of the problem-solving process. Also, in some cases, you may directly seek quick fixes to the problem without going into the reasons that caused the problem. For example, the problem might be that you get tired very soon. The normal tendency is to think that you are not getting proper sleep. But, in fact, the problem might not be lack of sleep; it may be due to some illness or stress. Thus, in this case, you wouldn't be able to solve your tiredness because you weren't addressing the right problem.

3. **Don't hurry up to solve the problem**
   There is a common tendency to try to solve it as quickly as possible. However, a more comprehensive approach would be to take time to find the right solution instead of jumping to the first possible solution that comes to your mind. And sometimes, by taking a break, we are able to look at the problem with a fresh mind and come up with some new insights.

4. **Don't be unnerved**

   It is natural that when a problem appears, we become panicky. But remember that a panic-ridden mind causes anxiety and seriously affects your ability to reach a clear and creative decision. A panicky mind also sends adrenaline across your body, making it difficult to think steadily and decisively. So, whenever faced with a problem, first, take a few deep breaths, go for a walk, or do whatever that relaxes you and allows you to regain your composure, and then approach the problem.

5. **Simplify problems**

   Problems are often complex. For example, if you are faced with a financial problem, you will have to think about many aspects of it, like not getting enough salary to meet your expenses, or you may be spending too much on unnecessary items, or not developing the necessary skills to get a better job. It would be easier to find a solution if you break the problem into its basic components and simplify it. You should focus on one step at a time rather than trying to fix everything at once.

6. **Think laterally**

   You may find yourself stuck in a catch-22 situation when you adopt the same approach to solving all your problems. For example, you may have tried to set up a business of your choice but were unable to succeed. But when you start thinking laterally, you open up your mind to different possible solutions and this helps you have more creative ideas. This way, you will be able to think of the businesses which are new and have less competition or select a market area where there is no business of that kind.

7. **Think of multiple solutions**

   An important aspect of problem-solving is to never dismiss an idea. Write down every possible solution to a problem you can think of. Sometimes, the ideas that seem weak initially can lead to or be adapted into a great idea. Also, thinking of multiple solutions will help you develop your problem-solving skills which will make you more effective at work, at home, and in your relationships.

Conclusion

Problem-solving and decision-making skills are not just abstract concepts but fundamental life competencies that shape our daily experiences. Throughout our exploration, we have unravelled the intricacies of these skills, discovering their profound impact on our personal and professional growth.

Problem-solving, we have learnt, is an art of its own. It entails more than just finding solutions; it's about identifying the right problems to solve and approaching them with creativity, resilience, and adaptability. Whether it's overcoming a complex challenge at work, navigating a personal crisis, or addressing societal issues, our ability to dissect problems and devise effective solutions is a testament to our resourcefulness.

Simultaneously, decision-making emerges as a critical juncture in our journey. Each decision we make carries the potential to achieve growth and success. It requires us to gather information, assess risks, and align our choices with our values. From choosing a career path to deciding on ethical dilemmas, our capacity to make sound decisions not only defines our character but also influences the world around us.

An important to realise here is that these skills are not isolated islands in our intellectual landscape; they are interconnected. Effective problem-solving informs better decision-making, and sound decisions often lead to more manageable problems. Together, they form a dynamic duo that empowers us to navigate the complex and ever-changing terrain of life. Furthermore, the ripple effect of our problem-solving and decision-making abilities extends far beyond our individual lives. They enable us to innovate, adapt, and collectively strive for a brighter future.

Chapter Nine

Stress Management

A few years back, a 12-year-old child, Amulya (name changed), came to Dr J. L. Kalra, a leading general practitioner in West Delhi, with his grandfather. The grandfather told the doctor that Amulya was not able to concentrate on his studies. On examination, Dr Kalra found that the child complained about seeing double images when he looked at an object. Dr Kalra then asked the child to walk up to the door, which was a few metres away, and come back as he wanted to check how he walked. The reason behind this test was that those who see double images walk very carefully because of the fear of falling. But in this case, the child was walking normally without any problem.

Dr Kalra was able to deduce that the child was perfectly fit and was lying to avoid studies. But before reaching a final conclusion, he wanted to confirm his prognosis by conducting a thorough check-up. He checked the child's vision, eye muscles, and fundus (the interior surface of the eye, opposite the lens) and found that everything was fine. Yet the child insisted he saw double images, one in front and one at the side. Dr Kalra then decided to treat him psychologically. He put an eye drop, just normal eye-refreshing drops, in the child's eyes and asked him to rest for 10 minutes with his eyes closed. He also told him that if he still saw double images, then an injection would be given in both eyes. After 10 minutes, the child informed that he was able to see properly.

Dr Kalra told the grandfather that the boy was alright but was over-stressed because of the pressure of his studies and instructed him not to make him study for more than an hour. He also told the child to play for an hour before going back to his studies and also give full attention to his studies.

* * *

The majority consensus is that stress is an enemy, and it needs to be avoided as much as possible. And everyone from spiritual teachers to personal coaches to dieticians has endless advice about how we can overcome stress. But what many of us don't know is that stress can also be a good and positive thing as it can motivate you to improve your focus, energy, and performance levels. At times, if the stress level is moderate, it can be exciting, bringing out the best in you as you would learn faster, would be more adaptable, and handle multiple tasks. In fact, if there were no stress, humankind wouldn't have survived. Nevertheless, bad stress must be avoided as it makes you feel uncomfortable and irritating, leading to a fall in your performance. It also increases anxiety levels which can result in more serious health issues.

But avoiding bad stress isn't as easy as it sounds in the current fast-paced hectic world and the more you try to avoid it, the more stressed you feel. Therefore, we need to deal with stress in a healthy manner and learn to manage it so that we do not suffer because of it. But before we look into the right way to respond to stress, let's get a better understanding of this phenomenon.

What Is Stress?

The term stress was conceptualised in 1936 by János Hugo Bruno Hans Selye CC, a pioneering Hungarian-Canadian endocrinologist, who defined it as 'the non-specific response of the body to any demand for change.'

In simple words, stress is primarily a physical response, i.e., it is the way your body and mind react to changes in life or particular situations and problems that create friction and are uncomfortable. Sadhguru Jaggi Vasudev, founder of the Isha Foundation, echoes a similar sentiment when he said that stress is like friction in a machine when there is no lubricant in it to function smoothly. It is the natural way the body reacts to a challenge and prepares the person to meet a tough situation with focus, strength, stamina, and heightened alertness.

But why has stress become such a predominant part of life and why does almost everyone complain of stress? The reason for its prevalence lies in a simple fact: our inability to manage our own system. This includes our body, mind, emotions, energy, and chemistry

How to Manage Stress?

Stress is a universal phenomenon and almost everyone faces it in varying degrees but some are more stress-prone than others because they are unable to manage it. Also, since it is a common happening and we are bound to come across some challenge or obstacle for sure on a regular basis that might elicit stress, it becomes important to get a better understanding of stress and how we can overcome it. If one is not able to do so, it can lead to severe consequences like anxiety, withdrawal, aggression, physical illness, and even addiction.

As mentioned, stress creates many changes in your mind and body to prepare you to respond to the arising danger or a situation. So, if we want to manage stress effectively, learning about its cause and mechanism might help but the most important way we can do so is by facing it boldly. When you decide to face the situation or problem head-on, you convince yourself that every problem has a solution, and that you can handle the situation effectively. The moment you decide to face the problem, your body and mind will undergo changes to help you relax and calm down. This 'relaxation response' would decrease your heart and breathing rate, develop a sense of well-being, and get better at managing stress.

Relaxation Response (RR)

Relaxation response is your ability to encourage your body to release chemicals and brain signals that make your muscles and organs slow down and increase blood flow to the brain. It is considered an effective response to a wide range of stress-related disorders and is the opposite reaction of the fight or flight response and neutralises its functional effects.

The fight or flight response is our body's natural reaction when we feel any excessive pressure, and it has been designed by nature to protect us from bodily harm. This response leads to a number of bodily changes such as increased metabolism, blood pressure, heart and breathing rate, dilation of pupils, and contraction of blood vessels, which, in turn, enable us to fight or flee from a stressful or dangerous situation. On the contrary, relaxation response is the deliberate effort to bring the body back to pre-stress levels by detaching from routine thought by choosing a word, sound, phrase, or prayer or by focusing on breathing. You can learn the RR technique by silencing your thoughts to create inner peace and better health.

The RR Technique

Sit in a comfortable position and close your eyes. Slacken your body, perceiving that all your muscles are relaxed. The process should begin from your feet and slowly progress upwards to the face. The entire body should be relaxed. When your body is completely relaxed, you should become aware of your breath coming in and out through your nose. Next, try to make your breathing easy and natural. Also, every time you breathe out, silently recite 'ommm'. Another point to keep in mind would be that the breathing-in time should be longer than the breathing-out time. This exercise should continue for 10 to 20 minutes. Initially, you may do it for 10 minutes and slowly increase to 20 minutes. You can use an alarm to indicate when the time is over.

When you have finished, sit quietly for five minutes in a squatting position and then slowly open your eyes and stand up. In the beginning, you may feel distracting thoughts, but you can train your mind to ignore them and keep your focus on your breath. Also, this exercise should be done after three hours of any meal and never after a full meal.

Yoga for Stress-Management

A number of studies have shown that yoga helps reduce stress and anxiety. It also enhances your mood and overall sense of well-being by improving your fitness along with balance, flexibility, range of motion, and strength in your body. By practising yoga, you can reduce risk factors for chronic diseases, such as heart disease and high blood pressure and alleviate chronic problems like depression, pain, anxiety, and insomnia. Being a mind-body practice, yoga is the best solution for stress management and a holistic health approach to help you achieve a peaceful body and mind.

Broadly, yoga covers three practices: posture, breathing, and meditation.

1. **Postures**

   Yoga postures or poses are a series of movements to increase the strength and flexibility of your body. Poses range from lying on the floor while completely relaxed to more difficult postures.

2. **Breathing**

   Controlling your breathing is an important part of yoga because it helps you be in command of your body and quieten your mind.

3. **Meditation**

   This involves practices such as mindfulness or focusing the mind on a particular object, thought, or activity to train attention and awareness and achieve a mentally clear and emotionally calm state. It helps to relax your body and mind and also helps you learn to be more mindful and aware of the present moment without being negative.

Precautions When Performing Yoga

Yoga is believed to be safe for healthy people. But in the beginning, it should be practised under the guidance of a trained instructor. It is also recommended to consult your doctor because, in some conditions, yoga might pose certain problems.

Yoga Postures for Reducing Stress

As we have covered, yoga poses, also known as *asanas*, can help with reducing stress and anxiety and strengthening the mind and body. Following are a few yoga exercises but we recommend that you either join a yoga class or engage a personal coach before undertaking any practice as they ensure that you perform each exercise properly, causing no damage to your body. Today, almost everywhere there are free yoga classes which one can apply for.

Now let's look at some yoga poses that can help to reduce stress.

1. **Sukhasana: Easy pose with a forward bend**

   This is a meditative pose and is the foundational exercise in yoga. The two basic requirements for this pose are flexible hips and a strong back. It acquires its name from two Sanskrit words: *sukh* which means easy and *asana* meaning posture. The purpose of this asana is to increase exhaling which causes a relaxation response. It is one of the simplest poses for meditation.

   How to Perform

   Sit on a mat on the floor with your legs stretched out. Fold the left leg and put it inside the right thigh. Then fold the right leg and put it inside the left thigh. Keep your hands on your knees. You should be sitting erect with your spine straight, distributing your weight evenly on the entire body. Hips should be balanced, aligning the head on the top of the spine so that bones have a firm foundation. This can be ensured by leaning backwards and forwards. Rest your hands on your thighs. The whole body should be relaxed, breathing should be normal, and the mind fixed between the two eyebrows.

Since it is the foundational asana, it helps in performing other more difficult asanas. It helps in toning and activating the central nervous system and helps in controlling blood pressure and heart palpitation. It also improves the digestive system because it increases blood supply to the stomach. This asana relaxes the brain, making your whole body and mind calm and stable. It not only strengthens the spine but also makes the back stronger and steadier and strengthens knees and ankles as well. However, sukhasana should be avoided by those who have hip and knee injuries or suffer from slip disc.

2. **Uttanasana: Standing forward bend with shoulder opener**

In uttanasana, 'ut' means power and 'tan' translates to stretch, extend, or lengthen out. This asana gives the spine a thoughtful and focused stretch and the deep forward bounce of the upper body, including the spine, opens the cramped muscles, boosts energy in the body, rejuvenates and revitalises cells, and provides more oxygen to the whole body.

How to Perform

Stand erect and firmly so that the feet and shoulder are parallel to each other. Bend down from the hips while keeping your waist. Also, while bending, knees should not be bent. Straighten out your legs slowly and lift your hips by pressing your heels into the ground. Stand straight and rest your hands on your hips. Inhale and exhale and gently relax your knees. While doing so, move your hips and tailbone slightly back so that the rest of your body moves forward.

Your knees should be relaxed, and your hands should rest on the ground, by the side of your feet and should be parallel to each other with second and middle toes pointing forward. Allow the chest to float over your feet, widening the space between your chest bone and pubis. Feel the bend and the stretch from your hip bone. Stretch should also be felt in your hamstrings and if it is not being felt, extend your knees a little more.

Turning the thighs inward and rooting yourself into your heels will allow better alignment. The head should droop in a way that the crown reaches the floor. Look through your legs and hold the pose.

To end the exercise, tighten the core and the abdomen muscles while inhaling and placing your hand on the hips. Rise slowly, ensuring there is a dilation in your back. Stand up slowly, maintaining a distance between your pubis and your chest bone.

3. **Prasarita Padottanasana: Wide-legged standing forward bend**

   'Prasarita' means wide or stretched out, 'pada' means foot, and 'uttana' means intense stretch. This is an excellent yogic exercise because it makes your body feel healed and expanded. This asana should be practised after doing standing poses and is a good foundation pose for inversions.

   How to Perform

   Begin the asana by standing at the front of your mat in the tadasana (mountain pose). Lightly move your feet apart anywhere from three to four-and-a-half feet, depending on your height. Keep your hands on your hips and ensure that the inner feet are parallel to each other. Now pull up your inner arches by drawing up on the inner ankles and pressing the outer edges of your feet and ball of the big toe firmly into the floor. Stretch your thigh muscles by drawing them up. Inhale while lifting your chest so that the front torso is slightly longer than the back.

   Now inhale and take a step backwards with your right foot so that your body faces the long edge of the mat. Now stretch your hands out at shoulder height and right above your feet. Then bring your hands to your hips and inhale, lengthening the chest and heart upwards so that your torso is stretched as well. Exhale and bend forward until your fingertips touch the mat in front of you. Continue to stretch, taking the top of your head to the ground and pushing the buttocks towards the ceiling. Involve your abdominal muscles with the lengthening of your spine. Then with elbows bent, keep your both hands either below your legs or next to your head. If it is comfortable, hold your big toes with your fingers. Maintain this pose for a minute, but if you cannot, reduce the time. Breathe deeply and slowly. Then, move your hands forward till the torso is parallel to the floor. Engaging your spine fully, move your hands to your hips and then inhale and lift up your torso. Come back to the tadasana.

4. **Sasangasana: Rabbit pose**

Sasangasana or the rabbit pose helps flex the spine, increase body awareness, relieve tension around the neck, and also keep hormones in control.

How to Perform

Sit on your heels, exhale all the air out, and hold your heels with the back of your hands facing out. Ensure that the thumbs are outside, and the fingers are inside. Next, by involving your core and lowering down, place the top of your head on the ground towards your knees in such a way that your forehead touches your knees. Now raise your hips high and roll forward like a wheel till your elbows are locked.

Then inhale deeply, pulling on your heels with a firm grip of your hands, followed by a deep exhale. Stay in this position for not less than five breaths and then slowly come up the same way you came in. Next, inhale and roll up one vertebra at a time with the chin and head coming up last. Make sure to never put much pressure on your head. Then clutch the lower of your feet and draw your shoulders away from your ears, making proper adjustments so that the crown of the head, and not the back of the head, is on the floor.

5. **Halasana: Plough pose**

Halasna boosts circulation, improves blood sugar levels and blood pressure, stretches the spine, tones muscles, and helps relieve tightness.

How to Perform

Lie down straight on the mat. Swing your legs back and over your head and rest your toes on the floor. Hold on for 10 breaths. Slowly roll out of this position, keeping your head back so that it doesn't hit forward when you bring your legs and torso back.

6. **Savasana: Corpse pose**

Savasana improves mental health and memory, lowers blood pressure, helps relax the body, and positively impacts the nervous system.

How to Perform

Lie down flat on your back without using cushions. If you do not feel comfortable, use a small pillow below your neck. Next, close your eyes and completely relax your feet and knees while keeping your legs apart and toes facing to the sides. Now place your arms sideways, a little spread apart from your body. Your palms should be open and face upward.

Now, shift your attention to different parts of your body one by one, slowly relaxing the entire body. Your awareness should begin with the right foot, moving on to the right knee, and so on. When you have completed one leg, shift your attention to the other leg and slowly move upwards to your head. Continue to breathe slowly but gently and deeply, so that the breathing relaxes you increasingly. The incoming breath will energise the body while the outgoing breath will bring relaxation. Remain in this position, free from all sense of hurry or urgency. You should be completely with your body, focusing on your breathing and ensuring that you do not fall asleep.

After about five minutes, slowly roll onto your right side, keeping your eyes closed. Remain in that position for a minute and then taking the support of your right hand, gently come to the sitting position. Keeping your eyes closed, take a few breaths, gradually becoming aware of your environment and the body. When you feel completely relaxed, slowly and gently open your eyes. This should be the last asana in your practice.

Importance of Yoga in the Corporate Sector

Corporate life is complex and full of challenges. Deadlines, office politics, peer pressure, pressure to perform, and long working hours, all this is a part of the life of every manager and member of the core management team. Working in a corporate industry also requires sitting for a long time in the office, attending prolonged meetings, and working long hours in front of the computer. All this leads to bad posture, mental fatigue, and several lifestyle diseases like diabetes, hyper-acidity, constipation, hypertension, and digestive issues. And if not addressed properly, it can lead to severe health issues like back pain, spondylitis, eye problems, insomnia, depression, headaches, obesity, pressure, diabetes, and other ailments. Generally, in such situations, doctors advise taking antibiotics and painkillers to manage these problems. But the fact is that such issues need to be dealt with properly and holistically.

In the 21st century, yoga is one of the best cures for these problems and illnesses. It is thus catching on and becoming highly popular in the corporate world. Many big corporate houses now provide in-office yoga classes for their employees because it helps to release stress. This activity is a win-win situation for both managers and owners because more relaxed and less stressed managers are more focused and productive and in turn, bring prosperity to the company.

Conclusion

Our voyage through the intricacies of stress management skills has illuminated a path towards greater resilience and well-being. Throughout this chapter, we have explored a tapestry of techniques and insights that empower us to navigate life's challenges with poise and equanimity. Stress, we have come to understand, is not an insurmountable force; it's a natural response to life's demands, and how we respond to it can make all the difference.

Our exploration has shown us that stress management is a holistic endeavour, encompassing physical, emotional, and mental dimensions. From mindfulness practices that ground us in the present moment to effective time management strategies, we have uncovered a rich tapestry of tools to help us regain control in the face of adversity. These skills, when woven together, create a safety net that cushions the impact of life's inevitable stressors.

Moreover, we have learned that stress is not inherently negative. It can be a motivator, a catalyst for growth, and a signal that we care deeply about what we do. By reframing our relationship with stress and viewing it as an opportunity for self-improvement, we harness its energy to fuel our personal development. By embracing these strategies and integrating them into our lives, we move closer to a state of balance, where stress becomes a manageable companion on the road to a fulfilling and harmonious existence.

Chapter Ten

Self-Control

It was a routine morning for news anchor Supreet Kaur when she began reading news on IBC24, a private television channel. A breaking news, in a live phone-in, came midway through the bulletin. She read out the news about a person dying in a road accident in a calm and composed manner. Though the phone-in did not name the victims, Supreet got an inkling from the make of the SUV—a Renault Duster—and the accident spot, at Pithora in Chhattisgarh's Mahasamund district, that the dying person was her husband. After finishing the bulletin, she rushed to the studio to confirm her worst fears. Her husband, Harsad Kawade, was one of the three dead. She broke down at this point and started calling relatives. Supreet and Harsad had been married for just about a year.

Though this case involved a tremendous tragedy, Supreet was able to not succumb to it in the moment. Like a true professional, she controlled her anxiety, remained fully composed, and showed exemplary commitment to her job.

This example highlights the importance of learning the skill of self-control. It is especially a powerful skill in any kind of professional setup as it brings more benefits and advantages in the long run than any other skill.

However, mastering the self is not an easy task as it needs much patience and intelligence.

In the following sections, we will explore this skill in more detail along with ways we can develop it.

* * *

What Is Self-Control?

Simply put, self-control is the ability to manage your impulses, emotions, and behaviours to achieve long-term goals. This crucial trait separates humans from animals as it gives us more autonomy on how we progress. Neuroscience has revealed that the prefrontal cortex (the part of the brain that plans, solves problems, and makes decisions) plays an important role in self-regulation. The richness of nerve connections in the prefrontal cortex enables us to plan and evaluate our actions. So, instead of being completely dominated by our immediate impulses, we can optimise our actions.

Why Is Self-Control Important?

'Like a city whose walls are broken down is a man who lacks self-control,' teaches the Bible. And this statement is very true because if you do not have self-control, you will face problems throughout your life.

Self-control is an essential skill for success. It allows us to concentrate our efforts and evaluate the best way forward to achieve our goals and aspirations. Not only that but it has also been shown that people who have better self-control lead a healthier and happier life. In an experiment conducted in the United States, students who exhibited greater self-control got better grades and higher test scores and were admitted in better academic programmes. It has also been found that self-control is a more important factor than IQ in academic success.

But the benefits of self-control go beyond academic performance. One research found that those who had high levels of self-control during childhood had high levels of physical and mental health in adulthood. It is also an important skill for self-development as it enables you to better deal with difficult situations, both in personal and professional settings. Your tolerance power and patience level will be low if you are unable to control your emotions and feelings. But if you have a high level of self-control, you will be more disciplined and have a better command over your life.

How to Develop Self-Control?

Given below are some steps that can help you master self-control.

1. **Avoid Temptation**

   One effective way to have better control over yourself is to avoid temptations and enticements. This can be achieved by finding a healthy distraction, for example going for a walk, calling a friend, or involving yourself in any activity to get your mind off temptations. Researchers at the University of Wyoming suggest that it is more effective to plan in advance on how to manage temptations. The following four strategies will help you resist temptations.

   First, as far as possible, avoid any situation that may tempt you. Second, if you cannot completely avoid a situation that may involve temptation, try to reduce the attraction. Third, divert your attention away from temptation. Fourth, change the way you think about the temptation so that it becomes less appealing. The fewer distractions you have, the more focused you will be on accomplishing your goals.

2. **Plan Ahead**

   Temptations can creep up suddenly without any warning. For example, you go to a friend's house and his mother has prepared all kinds of snacks that you like. If unprepared, the look and smell of food might break your determination. Therefore, you should plan in advance how you would keep any temptation that presents itself in check. It has been shown that planning in advance strengthens your willpower to foil temptations. For example, if you know that you crave food in the late afternoon, eat a well-balanced lunch full of fibre, protein, and whole grains to keep your hunger away for a longer time.

3. **Practice Self-Control**

   Self-control, like any other skill you want to master, requires regular practice to become better at it. So, try to regularly involve yourself in activities that require you to exert self-control. That will improve your willpower over time. The bigger the temptation, the more challenging and strenuous it will become to control your willpower. Thus, it is important to start with building your self-discipline through daily practice with smaller challenges. And with time, you will be able to handle bigger temptations without much effort.

4. **Know Yourself Better**

   An important part of self-control is knowing the self, and through introspection, we can better understand ourselves and know our strengths and weaknesses. This will allow us to develop a customisable plan to improve self-control.

5. **Learn New Things**

   Self-discipline is a vital part of the process whenever we pick up a new hobby or skill. Hence, by committing ourselves to a new skill, we would become better at self-control, as without it, we can only get so far.

6. **Find a Mentor**

   A mentor, coach, professional trainer, etc. can assist you in your journey to develop better self-control. Being accountable to someone else pushes us harder to be more disciplined. All successful leaders acknowledge the role of a mentor in developing their personality. The mentor will also give constructive feedback and guide you to achieve higher levels of performance.

7. **Exonerate Yourself and Move On**

   Despite your best intentions and well-laid plans, you might falter sometimes and give in to temptations. This is completely natural and whenever this happens, one should pick themselves up immediately and keep on moving forward. Do not sulk with guilt, anger, or frustration. These emotions will never help you and will only drag you further down and impede future progress. Thus, it is best to learn from your missteps and forgive yourself.

8. **Have a Technique**

   Whenever faced with a situation where you need to exert self-control, it is always advantageous to have some practice that can assist you in the process. For example, deep breathing is a popular way to centre yourself and prevent yourself from getting swayed by your emotions and feelings. It helps you to control yourself and better navigate difficult situations.

9. **Get Enough Sleep**

   Sleeping too late in the night causes sleep deprivation and it can weaken your self-control. Therefore, you must get enough sleep. It will keep you healthier in the long term and help you better manage your daily challenges.

Too Much Self-Control Can Be Harmful

So far, we have discussed the importance of self-control in achieving success on both professional and personal fronts. However, excessive self-control can actually be bad and harmful because it will make you risk-averse, overly cautious and tense, and less open to new avenues and prospects.

So even though it is important to have self-control, sometimes excessive levels of it can create problems. Therefore, developing a healthy balance of self-control is important to success as it will allow you to believe in your own abilities and overcome challenges and obstacles.

Conclusion

In conclusion, our journey through the complex terrain of self-control has uncovered not just a skill but a profound transformation of our inner selves. We have seen that self-control isn't merely about suppressing desires, but a mechanism for directing them towards our long-term ambitions. It serves as a bridge connecting who we are with who we aspire to be, empowering us to navigate life's unpredictable twists and turns with a sense of purpose and determination.

Our exploration has illuminated the dynamic nature of self-control. The strategies we have delved into, from setting clear intentions to fostering constructive habits, provide us with the means to nurture this essential skill, transforming it into a reliable compass guiding our daily decisions. And as we exercise self-control, we demonstrate dependability and discipline, earning the trust and respect of those around us.

Chapter Eleven

Multitasking

In the heart of Silicon Valley, a small startup named TechSolutions Inc. embarked on a journey that would test the limits of multitasking in the professional world. Founded by a dynamic duo, Alex and Sarah, this company embodied the importance of multitasking in the fast-paced realm of technology and innovation.

The story of TechSolutions began with a simple idea: to create a revolutionary software that would streamline communication between businesses and their customers. Alex, with his background in software development, and Sarah, a marketing genius, were the driving forces behind this vision. They knew that in order to succeed, they needed to wear multiple hats and seamlessly juggle various aspects of their burgeoning business.

In the early days, it was a two-person show. Alex would spend his mornings coding and developing the software, while Sarah hustled to secure partnerships and clients in the afternoons. Their evenings were dedicated to brainstorming strategies for growth. They soon realised that their ability to multitask was their secret weapon.

As the company expanded, so did the demands on Alex and Sarah's time. They hired a small team, but the startup culture meant that everyone needed to be versatile.

Meetings, presentations, coding, marketing, client relations—these tasks required careful coordination, and multitasking became an indispensable skill.

One pivotal moment came when TechSolutions secured a major contract with a Fortune 500 company. The client wanted the software customised to their unique needs, and the project was time-sensitive. Alex led the technical team, ensuring the code was modified accordingly, while Sarah managed the client relationship, providing real-time updates on the project's progress.

Amidst this, they received an urgent request from a potential investor. They couldn't afford to miss this opportunity, so Sarah put her marketing duties on hold and handled the investor meeting. Simultaneously, Alex addressed technical queries from their client, demonstrating their ability to multitask effectively in high-pressure situations.

TechSolutions' multitasking prowess didn't stop there. They expanded their services to include customer support. Sarah managed a team of customer service representatives, while Alex developed a chatbot to automate routine inquiries. Their multitasking abilities allowed them to handle diverse responsibilities, from team management to tech innovation.

The company's growth seemed unstoppable, but challenges emerged. A competitor threatened their market share, and they had to respond swiftly. Sarah launched a marketing campaign while Alex, working with the development team, added new features to the software. Their synchronised multitasking efforts resulted in a successful counter-attack, retaining their customer base and even attracting new clients. As TechSolutions continued to thrive, their story became an inspiration within the tech community. Their ability to manage multiple facets of their business was a testament to the importance of multitasking in the professional world. It wasn't about spreading oneself thin, but about using multitasking strategically to adapt, innovate, and excel in a competitive landscape.

Today, TechSolutions Inc. stands as a prominent tech company, and its founders, Alex and Sarah, have become multitasking icons. They exemplify the reality that in the ever-evolving world of business, those who can multitask effectively can navigate challenges, seize opportunities, and build empires.

The story of TechSolutions Inc. reminds us that in the professional world, multitasking isn't merely a skill; it's a superpower that empowers individuals and companies to conquer adversity, achieve greatness, and leave an indelible mark on their industry.

* * *

In our fast-paced modern world, the ability to multitask has become an essential skill. From the professional workplace to everyday life, multitasking plays a pivotal role in how we manage our time, accomplish tasks, and navigate the complexities of our interconnected lives. Multitasking, often touted as a desirable trait, is more than just juggling multiple tasks simultaneously. It encompasses a broad range of cognitive abilities, strategies, and behaviours that enable individuals to efficiently and effectively handle various demands in parallel.

In this comprehensive exploration, we delve deep into what is meant by multitasking skills and unravel the intricacies of this phenomenon. We will examine its various dimensions, cognitive processes, benefits, challenges, and real-world applications to gain a holistic understanding of this crucial skillset that has become indispensable in contemporary society.

The Essence of Multitasking

Multitasking, at its core, refers to the capacity to perform two or more tasks or activities concurrently. It is a mental skill that enables individuals to switch seamlessly between different tasks, allocate attention appropriately, and manage their time efficiently. However, the concept of multitasking goes beyond this basic definition, encompassing a multitude of aspects and nuances.

Types of Multitasking

Multitasking is not a one-size-fits-all skill. It comes in various forms, each requiring distinct cognitive abilities and strategies:

1. **Cognitive Multitasking**

   This involves performing multiple cognitive tasks simultaneously. For example, reading a book while listening to music or solving math problems while having a conversation with a friend.

2. **Task Switching**

   Task switching, often considered a subset of multitasking, refers to the ability to switch between tasks swiftly and efficiently. It includes the mental flexibility to transition from one task to another without losing focus or efficiency.

3. **Parallel Processing**

   Parallel processing involves executing multiple tasks that require different mental resources. For instance, a chef simultaneously manages multiple dishes on the stove while also coordinating the kitchen staff.

4. **Motor Multitasking**

   This type of multitasking involves coordinating physical actions simultaneously. Examples include driving a car while changing the radio station or playing a musical instrument.

5. **Information Multitasking**

   Information multitasking relates to managing and processing multiple streams of information simultaneously, such as monitoring social media while working or keeping track of multiple news sources.

6. **Interpersonal Multitasking**

   In interpersonal interactions, multitasking may entail listening to someone while formulating a response or engaging in active listening during a meeting while taking notes.

Cognitive Components of Multitasking

Multitasking skills draw upon several cognitive components, including:

1. Working Memory: The ability to hold and manipulate information temporarily is crucial

for keeping track of multiple tasks or goals simultaneously.
2. Attention Allocation: Effective multitasking requires allocating attention to different tasks in a way that maximizes productivity and minimizes errors.
3. Task Prioritisation: Recognising the relative importance and urgency of tasks is essential for multitasking effectively.
4. Task Coordination: Coordinating the timing and sequence of tasks is vital for preventing conflicts and optimising efficiency.
5. Task Monitoring: Continuous monitoring of the progress and status of ongoing tasks helps ensure that nothing is overlooked or neglected.

The Multifaceted Benefits of Multitasking

Multitasking skills, when applied judiciously, offer a range of benefits across various domains of life:

1. **Time Efficiency**

   Multitasking allows individuals to make the most of their time by accomplishing multiple tasks simultaneously. This is particularly valuable in a fast-paced work environment where time is a precious resource.

2. **Increased Productivity**

   Efficient multitaskers can tackle a broader range of tasks, boosting overall productivity. They can switch between tasks seamlessly, optimising their work output.

3. **Improved Task Management**

   Multitasking helps individuals manage their to-do lists effectively. It enables them to address urgent matters while also making progress on less time-sensitive tasks.

4. **Enhanced Problem-Solving**

   In some cases, multitasking can stimulate creative thinking and problem-solving. The ability to switch between tasks can lead to fresh perspectives and insights.

5. **Adaptability**

   Multitasking fosters adaptability, allowing individuals to respond swiftly to changing circumstances and unexpected challenges.

6. **Flexibility**

   A well-honed multitasking skillset equips individuals to handle diverse responsibilities and roles, making them versatile assets in various professional and personal contexts.

Developing Multitasking Skills: Strategies and Techniques

Multitasking is a skill that can be developed and refined over time through practice, awareness, and the application of effective strategies. Whether you are aiming to improve your multitasking abilities in the workplace, at home, or in various aspects of your life, here are several valuable techniques to help you become a more proficient multitasker:

1. **Prioritise Tasks**

   One of the keys to successful multitasking is understanding which tasks require your immediate attention and which can be deferred. Prioritisation allows you to allocate your focus to the most critical tasks while managing others in the background. Use techniques like the Eisenhower Matrix, which categorises tasks into four quadrants based on urgency and importance, to help prioritise effectively.

2. **Create To-Do Lists**

   Maintaining a comprehensive to-do list is an excellent way to keep track of tasks and ensure nothing is forgotten. Organise your list by priority and deadlines, and update it regularly. This practice not only helps you multitask efficiently but also reduces the mental burden of remembering every task.

3. **Set Clear Goals**

   Establish clear and specific goals for each task you are working on. Having a defined objective in mind makes it easier to maintain focus and track progress. Clearly defined goals can also help prevent distractions from derailing your efforts.

4. **Time Blocking**

   Allocate specific blocks of time to particular tasks or groups of related tasks. Time blocking helps you establish dedicated periods for focused work and allows you to structure your day for effective multitasking. Use digital calendars or planners to schedule and visualise your time blocks.

5. **Master Task Switching**

   Task switching is a fundamental aspect of multitasking. To switch tasks efficiently, practice transitioning smoothly between different activities. Minimise distractions during transitions, and avoid cognitive overload by allowing brief moments to refocus before moving on to the next task.

6. **Practice Cognitive Flexibility**

   Cognitive flexibility is the ability to shift your thinking and adapt to new information or tasks quickly. Engage in activities that challenge your cognitive flexibility, such as puzzles, brain teasers, or learning a new language. These exercises can enhance your capacity to switch between tasks seamlessly.

7. **Eliminate Unnecessary Distractions**

   Identify and eliminate distractions in your environment. Turn off notifications on your devices, close irrelevant tabs or applications, and create a dedicated workspace that minimises interruptions. A clutter-free environment can significantly enhance your multitasking efficiency.

8. **Use Technology Wisely**

   Technology can be both a boon and a bane for multitasking. Leverage productivity apps and tools to manage your tasks, set reminders, and automate routine activities. However, be mindful of over-reliance on technology, as it can contribute to distractions if not used judiciously.

9. **Multisensory Approach**

   Engage multiple senses to enhance your ability to multitask. For example, when learning a new skill or studying, combine reading with listening to audio resources or using visual aids. This multisensory approach can reinforce memory and understanding.

10. **Stay Organised**

    Maintain a well-organised workspace and digital filing system. A clutter-free environment reduces cognitive load, making it easier to manage multiple tasks effectively. Use digital tools like cloud storage and digital note-taking apps to keep your information organized and easily accessible.

11. **Practice Mindfulness**

    Mindfulness techniques, such as meditation and deep breathing exercises, can help improve your ability to concentrate and reduce stress. A calmer mind is better equipped to handle multiple tasks without feeling overwhelmed.

12. **Seek Feedback and Self-Reflection**

    Regularly seek feedback from colleagues, friends, or mentors on your multitasking abilities. Constructive feedback can help you identify areas for improvement. Additionally, engage in self-reflection to assess your multitasking performance, identify challenges, and adapt your strategies accordingly.

13. **Incremental Challenges**

    Gradually increase the complexity and number of tasks you attempt to multitask. Start with simpler combinations and progressively tackle more demanding scenarios. This incremental approach allows you to build confidence and competence over time.

14. **Learn from Experts**

    Observe individuals known for their multitasking skills, whether they are colleagues, mentors, or public figures. Analyse their techniques, strategies, and habits to glean insights that you can apply to your own multitasking endeavours.

15. **Practice, Practice, Practice**

    Like any skill, multitasking improves with practice. Regularly challenge yourself to multitask in controlled settings. Experiment with different combinations of tasks and gradually refine your approach based on your experiences.

Remember that developing multitasking skills is a continuous process. It requires patience, self-awareness, and adaptability. What works best for one person may not be the most effective approach for another, so be willing to experiment and tailor your strategies to your unique strengths and challenges. With dedication and perseverance, you can become a more proficient and efficient multitasker, enhancing your productivity and effectiveness in various aspects of your life.

Conclusion

In this chapter, we have explored strategies, tools, and techniques for mastering the art of multitasking. From the workplace to daily life, multitasking stands as both a formidable ally and a potential challenge. We also learnt that multitasking is not a one-size-fits-all endeavour. It adapts to the unique demands of different professions, life situations, and individual preferences. The skills required to master multitasking are varied, encompassing cognitive abilities, time management, goal setting, and adaptability.

As we conclude this chapter, let us remember that mastering multitasking is not a destination but an ongoing process of growth and refinement. It requires self-awareness, practice, and an openness to adapt to evolving circumstances and work environments.

As you move forward in your personal and professional endeavours, may this understanding of multitasking serve as a compass, guiding you to navigate the complexities of a multitasking landscape, achieve your goals, and find fulfilment in your diverse pursuits.

Chapter Twelve

Emotional Quotient (EQ)

Renu had an IQ of 162 and was a brilliant student. During her school days, while other girls joined dance classes and enjoyed their evenings, Renu spent most of her time in her study room. Due to this reason, she did not have many friends and was not popular. By isolating herself, she found it increasingly difficult to develop relationships with anyone.

Deenu, who was Renu's classmate, was completely opposite of Renu. He brimmed with magnetism and was popular among students. Being extroverted, expressive, and friendly, he always attracted everyone. Though an average student, he was able to take on any challenge that life threw at him.

A few years later, Renu was selected for AIIMS and after getting her MD, she began practising medicine. However, she continued to have difficulty in forming close relationships with people. She later got married but it ended in divorce. Deenu passed out from Sri Ram College of Commerce and started his own business. Today he is a successful entrepreneur with a happily married life. He has a loving wife and three children.

Though both are success stories, according to you, who had a more fulfilling life, Renu or Deenu? The answer is that even though Renu had a higher IQ, Deenu was able to lead a more social and fulfilling life due to his ability to form connections with other people and relate to them on a deeper level. And this has been the case with many leaders and highly successful people. The late president, Ronald Reagan, was not as educated as many of his colleagues, but he left them behind by having an intensely charming personality. And it was his charm and his ability to relate to people that made him one of the most popular and successful presidents of the United States. Thus, from this example, we can deduce that how you emotionally relate to people plays a more important role than your intelligence level.

***

Only a few decades back, intelligence quotient (IQ) was the sole determining factor for gauging how successful a person would be, but this is not the case anymore. The reason for this is that IQ only indicates the intelligence level and not the emotional skills of a person. And now we know that this skill, known as emotional quotient (EQ), is essential to succeed in present-day society. This is because people with high emotional intelligence or EQ, regulate and identify their own emotions and also better understand the emotions of others. In other words, it is your ability to observe and manage your own and other people's sentiments by distinguishing between different emotions and labelling them appropriately. This, in turn, allows you to use this emotional information to guide your thinking and behaviour. Therefore, a strong EQ in you is *sine qua non* for better mental health, improved job performance, and better leadership skills.

Let's explore this further.

What Is EQ?

As mentioned, emotional quotient, also known as emotional intelligence quotient, measures your sensitivity towards your as well as other people's emotions. This ability to properly interpret, evaluate, regulate, and manage emotions plays a crucial role in navigating through all kinds of situations and environments. Moreover, it allows you to be more socially involved and build strong relationships.

Why Is EQ Essential for Success?

Though the concept of EQ was first introduced way back by Michael Beldoch, who was a clinical professor of psychology in psychiatry at Weill Cornell Medical College, New York City, it was only taken seriously when Daniel Goleman, a science journalist, published a book proving that EQ was more important than IQ when it came to success and leadership. He showed that conventional intelligence, as measured by IQ, is indicative of only cognitive reasoning ability and emotional intelligence was a more accurate indicator of whether a person will go on to be a successful working professional because, in every profession, human interaction is integral and unavoidable.

Several studies in recent years have confirmed the correlation between EQ and success. The results revealed that persons with high EQ performed better in the workplace, proved better leaders, and were more self-confident, trustworthy, and more likeable than those with low EQ. This shows that EI is more important than IQ.

Let's now look at the areas that are affected when a person has higher EQ:

1. **Overall Health**

   Emotional quotient is a strong determining factor in how you care for your overall health. If you cannot manage your emotions, it will lead to serious health problems. Only if you are able to control your emotions can you maintain good health.

2. **Happiness**

   Uncontrolled emotions can affect mental health and cause anxiety and depression. And since EQ also plays a crucial role in developing relationships with others, without it, one can end up lonely and isolated, which in turn would affect one's attitude and outlook towards life. Thus, a person with high EQ will be more likely to have a positive attitude and happier outlook.

3. **Relationships**

   Understanding and controlling emotions enables you to understand others better and also express yourself more efficiently This provides for effective communication and builds stronger relationships both in the office and family.

4. **Conflict Resolution**

   It is easier to resolve conflicts when you can perceive the emotions of others and understand their perspectives. Negotiations become easy when you are able to understand the needs and desires of others. Therefore, with high EQ, it becomes easier to solve the issue.

5. **Leadership**

   Building strong bonds with team members makes a leader more successful and effective. If you can understand what motivates your co-workers, communicate with them in a positive way, and utilise their emotional diversity, then you can achieve better results as a team. And to do so, your EQ level needs to be high.

Developing Higher EQ

Research by the Carnegie Institute of Technology, Pittsburgh, Pennsylvania, emphasised that, on an average, the role of academic knowledge made up only for 15 per cent of a successful person's character traits, while the remaining 85 per cent consisted of human engineering skills like personality, ability to communicate, negotiate, and leadership qualities. This means that you can become a leader in your field and earn more money and fame only if you develop a high EQ during your formative years. This is because high EQ would enable you to become a better communicator, develop strong relationships, and successfully negotiate tricky situations. Not only that, but a higher EQ will also mean that you will be kind-hearted and compassionate to your friends and colleagues in your social life and to your spouse and children at home. Therefore, it is important to make efforts to raise the level of your EQ.

Developing high EQ has become more important nowadays because the education system is strongly focused on improving intellectual ability only. The following methods will help you improve your EQ level.

1. **Recognise Your Emotions**

   You should learn to identify emotions by naming the emotion, whether it is happiness or anger. This will allow you to better understand the nuances of your emotions and also the cause that triggers them. Also, by nurturing a better relationship with your own emotions, you will be able to better understand what others are feeling and how it affects them.

2. **Have an Open-Mind**

   Having a mind with rigid opinions and a narrow outlook prevents one from properly understanding and considering different ideas or views. Such a mind is biased and intolerant of new perspectives. An open mind, on the other hand, is willing to consider different ideas and understand various aspects of a problem without any predetermination and accordingly work out an effective solution. This quality will make you a person who is open to diverse ideas and opinions and enable you to think critically and logically.

3. **Active listening**

   An important part of EQ is giving due space to others to express their opinion and feelings. Hence, paying attention to what someone is saying and actively and intensely listening to them is a habit that we should inculcate. Active listening will make people feel that they are being heard and being taken seriously. Using eye contact, nodding your head to acknowledge, and asking questions like 'What was that you liked?' or 'How did that make you feel?' are some additional aspects of active listening.

4. **Nurture Self-Awareness**

   Becoming more self-aware and sensitive to your emotions will make you better at managing your emotions. This is possible when you nurture your emotions by recognising them, examining them, and considering stimulating points. It will also make you aware of other people's emotions and better understand their stance.

5. **Understand All Viewpoints**

   After having a good assessment of your own emotions, you should try to understand the emotions of others and empathise with them. Try to understand how they may have reached their conclusions and develop a broader perspective, or else you will be unnecessarily insisting on your own viewpoint every time.

6. **Communicate Effectively**

   Communication, both verbal and non-verbal, depends on how well you understand the emotions as well as the intentions of other people. This allows you to find a relatable and common ground and get your point across more effectively.

7. **Emotional Management**

   An important step for effective emotional management is that we should not be in a hurry to process and understand what is happening and wait till we are more composed to better analyse the situation. We can go for a walk, exercise, play with a pet, or breathe deeply, and afterwards come back to the issue at hand. Looking at the bigger picture will help us make more informed decisions.

These are the various ways to improve your EQ which, in turn, will assist you in your career and lead to better relations, both personal and professional.

Conclusion

Though it might seem that in order to reach a higher rung on the career ladder, one needs to be ruthless and stone-hearted, the truth is far from this. Some of the most successful CEOs in the world are level-headed leaders who know how to use emotional intelligence to bring out the best in themselves as well as those working with or for them. These are the best examples of business leaders who have not only achieved success but have earned the respect of the people they work with.

Overall, emotional intelligence plays a crucial role in all spheres of life as it necessitates understanding self and others. Therefore, you should make emotional intelligence a lifelong objective and keep working on it.

Chapter Thirteen

Negotiation Skills

Our story takes us back to the early 2000s when a small, family-owned manufacturing company named InnovateTech faced a dire predicament. InnovateTech specialised in producing cutting-edge components for the automotive industry. However, as the industry underwent rapid technological advancements, InnovateTech found itself grappling with obsolescence and dwindling revenues.

Desperate to secure its future, the company's leadership decided on a bold and audacious plan—to pivot into producing components for the emerging electric vehicle (EV) market. They believed that this pivot was their only chance for survival, but there was a massive hurdle; they needed a substantial injection of capital to retool their manufacturing processes and develop EV-compatible components.

Enter David Martinez, a seasoned venture capitalist known for his sharp negotiation skills and knack for identifying diamonds in the rough. InnovateTech's executives reached out to Martinez in the hopes of securing a substantial investment to fund their transformation.

The negotiation began with InnovateTech's leadership presenting their ambitious vision for the company's future. They detailed their market research, prototypes, and projections for the EV market's growth. However, Martinez, shrewd and pragmatic, was not easily convinced. He knew the risks involved in backing a struggling company with an unproven pivot strategy.

Over a series of meetings and negotiations, David Martinez meticulously assessed the situation. He probed every aspect of InnovateTech's business plan, scrutinising their financials, competitive positioning, and leadership team. But it was his negotiation finesse that truly shone.

Recognising the desperation in InnovateTech's plea, Martinez approached the negotiation table with empathy. He understood that the success of this negotiation was not only a financial gain but also a lifeline for a struggling business. He skilfully balanced the need for a favourable investment deal with the need to maintain the company's integrity and control.

The negotiation was intense, marked by debates over-valuation, equity stakes, and the terms of the investment. InnovateTech's leadership was adamant about retaining a significant portion of ownership to maintain their vision. Martinez, on the other hand, sought to mitigate his risks while providing the necessary capital.

In the end, after months of negotiations and revisions to the terms, a deal was struck. David Martinez agreed to invest a substantial sum in InnovateTech, securing a minority equity stake. The terms allowed InnovateTech's leadership to maintain operational control while providing the company with the financial resources needed to transition successfully into the EV component market.

The impact of this negotiation was transformative. InnovateTech used the investment to retool its facilities, develop innovative EV components, and position itself as a key player in the burgeoning electric vehicle industry. Over the years, the company not only survived but thrived, eventually going public and becoming a market leader in its sector.

This real-life business story underscores the paramount importance of negotiation skills in the professional world. David Martinez's negotiation finesse, marked by empathy, strategic thinking, and a commitment to win-win outcomes, not only saved a struggling company but also paved the way for its remarkable success in a rapidly evolving industry. It serves as a testament to the notion that effective negotiation can be the crucial factor for unlocking opportunities and achieving mutually beneficial solutions in the complex and ever-changing landscape of business.

* * *

Negotiation is the cornerstone of human interaction, a fundamental skill that transcends borders, industries, and contexts. It is a dynamic and intricate process that shapes the outcomes of our personal and professional lives. Whether securing a business deal, resolving a dispute, navigating a complex relationship, or even haggling at a local market, negotiation plays an integral role in achieving our objectives, big or small.

In the world of business, politics, law, and everyday affairs, negotiation is often the difference between success and failure. It is a skill that can be honed and mastered, and its significance cannot be overstated. This chapter serves as a comprehensive exploration of negotiation skills, delving into what it encompasses, why it is vital in various aspects of life, and how it can be developed to succeed on a professional front.

Defining Negotiation Skills

Negotiation skill, at its core, is the art and science of reaching agreements between parties with differing interests, needs, and perspectives. It is the ability to navigate the complexities of conflicting desires and find common ground, often in the pursuit of shared objectives. At its essence, negotiation is a dynamic conversation where parties seek to influence each other's decisions to achieve a desirable outcome.

The term 'negotiation skills' encompass a broad spectrum of competencies and attributes that enable individuals to excel in the negotiation process. These skills are multifaceted, comprising both tangible and intangible qualities. Here, we delve into the various elements that constitute negotiation skills:

1. **Communication Skills**
   Effective communication is the backbone of negotiation. It involves the capacity to articulate thoughts clearly, listen actively to the other party, and express ideas persuasively. Communication skills encompass verbal and nonverbal communication, tone, body language, and the ability to convey information effectively.

2. **Emotional Intelligence**
   Emotional intelligence, often referred to as EQ, is the ability to recognise, understand, and manage one's own emotions and the emotions of others. In negotiation, EQ enables individuals to empathise

with the other party, gauge their emotional state, and respond with tact and sensitivity. It is essential for building rapport and fostering cooperation.

3. **Active Listening**

   Active listening involves not only hearing the words spoken but also comprehending the underlying message, intent, and emotions. Effective negotiators are skilled at active listening, allowing them to uncover hidden interests, concerns, and opportunities for collaboration.

4. **Problem-Solving and Critical Thinking**

   Negotiation often involves complex issues and challenges. Problem-solving and critical thinking skills are essential for analysing situations, identifying potential solutions, and making informed decisions that benefit all parties.

5. **Creativity and Flexibility**

   Successful negotiators think outside the box and approach problems with creativity and flexibility. They are open to alternative solutions and are willing to adapt their strategies to changing circumstances.

6. **Patience and Persistence**

   Negotiations can be protracted and require patience to navigate impasses and overcome obstacles. Persistence is necessary to stay focused on the ultimate goal and to continue seeking mutually beneficial agreements.

7. **Empathy**

   Empathy involves understanding and appreciating the feelings, needs, and perspectives of the other party. It allows negotiators to build trust, find common ground, and forge meaningful connections.

8. **Conflict Resolution**

   Conflict is inherent in negotiation. The ability to manage and resolve conflicts constructively is a critical skill for negotiators. It involves finding win-win solutions that address differences while preserving relationships.

9. **Preparation and Research**

   Thorough preparation and research are the foundation of effective negotiation. This includes gathering information about the other party, understanding the issues at stake, and formulating a negotiation strategy.

10. **Ethical Considerations**

    Ethical considerations in negotiation involve maintaining honesty, integrity, and fairness throughout the process. Ethical negotiators adhere to principles of transparency and avoid manipulation or unethical tactics.

Negotiation skills are a dynamic interplay of these attributes. The specific mix of skills and qualities required can vary depending on the negotiation context and the parties involved. Furthermore, negotiation skills are not solely about achieving a favourable outcome for oneself but also about creating value and fostering positive relationships. The ability to find win-win solutions is a hallmark of masterful negotiation.

The Ubiquity of Negotiation Skills

Negotiation skills are not confined to formal negotiations at the conference table. Its ubiquity is evident in various facets of life, where individuals engage in negotiations daily, often without realizing it. Here are some common scenarios where negotiation skills are indispensable:

1. **Business Negotiations**
   In the corporate world, negotiations occur at every level, from high-stakes mergers and acquisitions to day-to-day vendor contracts and employee discussions. Business leaders must possess negotiation skills to secure deals, resolve disputes, and manage relationships with stakeholders.

2. **Conflict Resolution**
   Whether in personal relationships, workplace conflicts, or international diplomacy, the ability to negotiate effectively is essential for resolving disputes and finding common ground.

3. **Sales and Marketing**
   Sales professionals use negotiation skills to understand customer needs, address objections, and close deals. Marketing teams negotiate partnerships and collaborations to expand reach and influence.

4. **Human Resources**

   HR professionals negotiate employment contracts, compensation packages, and employee benefits. They also mediate workplace conflicts and facilitate discussions between parties with differing interests.

5. **Legal Profession**

   Attorneys are skilled negotiators who advocate for their clients' interests in legal matters, including settlements, contracts, and litigation.

6. **Everyday Life**

   In daily life, individuals negotiate with family members, friends, and acquaintances on matters ranging from household chores to vacation planning.

Given the ubiquitous nature of negotiation, the ability to negotiate skilfully has a far-reaching impact on an individual's personal and professional success. Whether it involves achieving financial objectives, building meaningful relationships, or resolving conflicts, negotiation skills are a powerful tool in the toolkit of life.

Why Negotiation Skills Matters

The significance of negotiation skills extend beyond individual transactions or interactions. It has broader implications for organisations, communities, and society as a whole. Here are some compelling reasons why negotiation skills matter:

1. **Economic Impact**

   Effective negotiations lead to favourable outcomes, such as profitable business deals, cost savings, and increased revenue. Conversely, poor negotiation can result in financial losses and missed opportunities.

2. **Conflict Resolution**

   Negotiation is a peaceful and constructive means of resolving conflicts. It reduces the likelihood of disputes escalating into confrontations or legal battles.

3. **Innovation and Problem-Solving**

   Negotiation encourages creative problem-solving. It requires parties to think critically and explore alternative solutions, leading to innovative outcomes.

4. **Organisational Effectiveness**

   In the corporate world, negotiation skills are essential for effective leadership, employee management, and stakeholder relations. Leaders who negotiate skilfully can drive organizational success.

5. **Global Diplomacy**

   On the international stage, diplomacy and negotiations play a pivotal role in maintaining peace, resolving conflicts, and advancing global interests.

6. **Personal Empowerment**

   Individuals who possess negotiation skills are better equipped to assert their interests, advocate for their needs, and achieve personal goals.

7. **Social Impact**

   Negotiation skills can be used to address social issues, such as community development, nonprofit initiatives, and social justice advocacy.

In essence, negotiation skills are a catalyst for positive change. It empowers individuals and organisations to navigate complex challenges, seize opportunities, and contribute to the betterment of society. As a tool for achieving win-win outcomes, negotiation skills align with the principles of fairness, cooperation, and value creation.

Developing Negotiation Skills

Negotiation skills are not innate; it is a skill that can be developed and refined through learning, practice, and experience. Whether you are a seasoned professional or someone embarking on their negotiation journey, there are several avenues to enhance and leverage your negotiation skills:

1. **Education and Training**

   Formal education and training programs in negotiation provide valuable insights and techniques. These programs offer structured approaches to negotiation and allow participants to practice in controlled environments.

2. **Real-World Experience**

   Hands-on experience in negotiations is invaluable. Engaging in negotiations at work, in personal relationships, or through volunteer opportunities provides practical exposure and opportunities for growth.

3. **Mentorship and Coaching**

   Mentorship by experienced negotiators or coaching from negotiation experts can accelerate skill development. Learning from those who have mastered the art of negotiation provides valuable insights and guidance.

4. **Self-Study and Resources**

   A wealth of books, articles, podcasts, and online resources are available on the subject of negotiation. Self-study allows individuals to explore various negotiation strategies and techniques.

5. **Simulation and Role-Playing**

   Participating in negotiation simulations and role-playing exercises allows individuals to practice negotiation scenarios and experiment with different approaches.

6. **Feedback and Reflection**

   Reflecting on past negotiations and seeking feedback from peers or mentors can uncover areas for improvement. Self-awareness is a critical component of skill development.

7. **Networking**
   Engaging with a diverse network of professionals provides exposure to different negotiation styles and approaches. Networking also offers opportunities for collaborative negotiations and partnerships.

8. **Cross-Cultural Competence**
   In a globalised world, understanding and respecting cultural differences is essential for successful negotiations. Cross-cultural training enhances the ability to navigate diverse negotiation contexts.

9. **Technology and Tools**
   Utilising negotiation software and digital tools can streamline the negotiation process and provide data-driven insights for decision-making.

The development of negotiation skills require adaptability and a willingness to learn from both successes and failures. Additionally, negotiation is a dynamic field that evolves alongside changes in society, technology, and business practices. Staying informed about emerging trends and best practices is essential for staying at the forefront of negotiation skills.

Conclusion

Negotiation skills are a multifaceted discipline that holds the keys to unlocking opportunities, resolving conflicts, and achieving success in various aspects of life. By gaining a comprehensive understanding of negotiation skills, from the fundamentals to advanced techniques, we can equip ourselves with the knowledge and confidence to negotiate effectively, whether in the boardroom, the living room, or the global arena.

Chapter Fourteen

Social Skills

Social skills play an important part in achieving career goals, developing personality, and expanding professional network. Therefore, understanding and improving your social skills can benefit you throughout your life. But first, let's explore what is implied by social skills.

Social skills, also known as interpersonal skills or soft skills, are how you communicate with others in society. These skills, verbal and non-verbal, help in interaction and communication with others in the office, family, neighbourhood, etc., in a variety of ways. The verbal aspect involves the spoken language, while non-verbal communication includes body language, facial expressions, and eye contact.

Social skills are important because every time you interact with others, you use social skills in one way or the other. With strong social skills, you can maintain and develop successful relationships, personally and professionally. These skills help you to communicate more effectively and efficiently, develop, maintain, and nurture your relationships as well as build new contacts. These skills are important no matter in what position and industry you are working in.

Types of Social Skills

As mentioned, well-developed social skills are an essential requirement to grow in your personal and professional lives. Enriched with social skills, you can develop better relationships, negotiate difficult social situations, communicate clearly and effectively, further your career, and feel happier.

In the professional sphere, these skills provide support in difficult or hard-to-navigate situations, expand your network, and make the workplace more enjoyable. Some of the important social skills include:

1. **Written Communication**

   This skill enables you to share your thoughts and ideas clearly and explain projects and goals to your team in writing. In today's workplace, you regularly send emails, make presentations, and write a lot. You can convey your thoughts in an easy-to-understand manner by improving your written communication skills. For a better writing strategy, you should focus on areas you want to improve. For example, you may benefit from reading more and paying particular attention to style and grammar. Wide reading will also help you develop a stronger vocabulary, helping you in better articulation of your thoughts and ideas. Try developing your own written communication style. Resumes and cover letters are also opportunities for you to display your social skills through your writing ability.

2. **Non-verbal Communication**

   As the name describes, non-verbal communication consists of communicating without the use of language. When communicating, we also give out signals about our emotional state and internal thoughts through our body language. For example, your body language can indicate how attentively you are speaking or listening. Eye contact is another important non-verbal communication as it shows that you are attentively listening to the person. Eye contact of three to five seconds before looking away is considered good. You should also often nod your head to show that you are listening and understanding what the person saying. These indirect signals will give the person a positive feedback and help him express his thoughts more easily.

3. **Conflict Resolution**

   The ability to reach a common ground among people who hold different opinions, goals, or ways of working is referred to as a conflict resolution skill. This skill is crucial as it makes the workplace a more friendly place and helps maintain the morale of the team. To get better at conflict resolution, you should try to understand the perspectives of different people or groups and ensure that your team reaches a consensus that satisfies everyone. The truth is that disagreements and dissatisfaction are bound to arise in the working environment and thus, conflict resolution is an important skill to have.

4. **Empathy**

   It is the ability to recognise emotions or state of mind of other persons. By better understanding the emotions and feelings of your colleagues and clients, you can relate to them and make decisions accordingly. Also, if you are empathetic to others, they will have confidence in you which, in turn, would enable you to build stronger, more respectful, and open relationships with them. Companies value empathetic people because they build an inspiring and healthy social environment.

5. **Emotional Intelligence**

   It is the ability to regulate your emotions. Effective handling of your emotions enhances your ability to work and develops more compassionate relationships with others. Also, your ability to identify your own emotions will enable you to connect with others as well. You can increase your emotional intelligence by having an awareness of your feelings in a particular situation.

6. **Positivity**

   Having a positive attitude will generate a healthy environment at your workplace and create a conducive work culture. That is the reason why employers always prefer people who are self-motivated, confident, and eager to work. They prove to be excellent leaders and are always an asset to their organisation. One effective way to develop positivity is to appreciate and praise other people for their achievements and accomplishments.

7. **Cooperation**

   Cooperation is essential for a productive and harmonious work environment. It encourages idea-sharing and develops creative solutions to problems. Cooperation and teamwork are valuable skills as every employer prefers those who can motivate others to give their best to the work.

An important aspect of improving your social skills is to put the above-mentioned skills into practice at home and work. Also never miss volunteer opportunities or extra-curricular activities where you can practice interpersonal skills.

Improving Social Skills

For some people, social skills come naturally but that's not the case with the majority. The good news is that with consistent effort, anyone can improve their social skills. Some of the tips to keep in mind have been mentioned below.

The first step to improve your social skills is pretty simple and it consists of observing others—family members, friends, and colleagues—who are gifted with strong social skills. By noticing how they use these skills, you can pick up their techniques and very soon you will be able to use them as naturally as they do. The second step would be to actively get involved with people who have good social skills. This way, you will first-hand demonstration of how these skills can be put into practice. The third step would be to get familiar with popular and relevant topics as it makes it easier to converse and connect with others. The fourth step is to listen carefully when others are speaking and speak intelligently and clearly when you get the chance to speak. Respond to what they have said and speak in a clear and confident voice. Lastly, be mindful of how you carry yourself as this too makes a significant impact on other people.

Conclusion

Social skills are a complex combination of abilities and behaviours but with enough practice and time, anyone can improve these skills. Ultimately, your goal should be to learn how to use social skills to develop and maintain close relationships with others, which can benefit you in a variety of ways. We can end this chapter with the timeless Turkish proverb that sophisticatedly states: 'No road is long with good company.'

Chapter Fifteen

Traits for Success

Congratulations on reaching the end of the book. We have covered all the essential skills that you would require to become a highly successful global leader like Sundar Pichai of Google, Satya Nadella of Microsoft, Ajay Banga of Mastercard, Indira Nooyi of PepsiCo, Ivan Menezes of Diageo, and Shantanu Naraye of Adobe Systems. In this chapter, we won't focus on a specific skill but instead, look at some general traits of some of the most successful leaders in the world.

Richard St. John, an American success expert, provides elucidating research on the common traits found in most successful corporate leaders in his aptly title book, *The 8 Traits Successful People Have in Common.* For this study, John interviewed more than 500 highly successful people, from Bill Gates and Richard Branson to Martha Stewart and Ben Cohen, the co-founder of Ben and Jerry's ice cream. His main finding was that success was a continuous journey and that each person's path to success was unique, but there were many commonalities among the world's most successful people. These eight common traits that he identified are as follows:

1. Be passionate about your work
2. Work hard but enjoy it

3. Have a definite focus:
4. Pull out of your comfort zone
5. Incessantly find new ideas
6. Keep on improving
7. Provide value to others
8. Be untiring through failure

Another study, by Brian Tracy, a Canadian-American motivational public speaker and self-development author, focused on the behaviour and habits of highly successful people. He has identified seven habits that you need to develop if you want to reach the top of your career.

1. **Be goal-oriented**

   You should develop the habit of working with clear goals and definite plans. In fact, every day of the work should be well planned. All highly successful people are passionately goal-oriented. They know exactly what they want and develop written plans to accomplish it.

2. **Be result-driven**

   Being result-driven requires setting very clear priorities and then concentrating single-mindedly on the most valuable use of your time. All successful people manage their time in such a way that their work output is efficient.

3. **Be action-oriented**

   It is essential to implement your ideas and plans in the most effective and efficient manner in order to achieve the desired result. This requires one to the nurture habit of being action-oriented which is the ability to get on with the job and get it done fast.

4. **Be people-oriented**

   The fourth habit consists of developing healthy relationships with the team and colleagues. For this, one needs to inculcate qualities such as patience, kindness, compassion, and understanding. All these qualities enable you to get along well with other people.

5. **Be physically fit**

   Good health is the most important element of success. This can be done by fastidiously watching your diet and exercising on a regular basis. Also, you must take proper rest and spend good time in recreational activities to enable you, in combination with diet and exercise, to live a healthy life.

6. **Never be dishonest**

   The sixth aspect is striving for honesty and integrity. The character you develop as you go through your life is more important than virtually anything else. Thus, it is important to develop a vision for yourself and then live your life by these highest ideals. This attitude of honesty and never compromising your integrity is critical for success.

7. **Have a high degree of self-discipline**

   Self-discipline is the ability to resist impulses, maintain focus, and see projects through to completion. Self-discipline at work will not only allow you to give your full attention to the task at hand but will also make you more diligent and engaged with your work.

ACKNOWLEDGEMENTS

The idea of this book, *From 9 to Success: Mastering Skills for the Global Work Ecosystem*, came up during my interactions with the students of Lal Bahadur Shastri Institutes of Management at New Delhi and Bareilly, Pioneer Business School, and Sri Sharada Institute of Indian Management-Research, New Delhi. A question that was often asked was: 'How to get good jobs in multinational companies?' I then suggested the management to organise a few general lectures on developing skills for getting good jobs in global companies. Many lectures I gave in the following years greatly helped students. A number of them sent me emails thanking me for helping them to develop skills that make them highly successful. They also suggested that I develop those lectures into a book so that a large number of young aspiring students can benefit. This book is the product of their suggestion which, I hope, would benefit those aspiring for good jobs and prosperous life. I am thankful to all those students who gave the idea for this book.

I am thankful to my daughter, Monika, and son-in-law Gautam, both authors of best-selling books, for always motivating me to remain busy intellectually. Their provocation made this book possible. My granddaughter, Meera, has been a source of inspiration and strength to me. An affectionate love to her. My wife, Mridula, when she was alive, read and reread the manuscripts of many chapters, gave valuable inputs, and helped me improve them. This book is because of her. May her soul rest in peace.

Special thanks to Aditya Jarial, associate editor at Hay House Publishers (India) Pvt Ltd, for perceptively and painstakingly editing the book which greatly enhanced its quantity, making it more readable. Finally, thanks to those numerous friends and colleagues for giving me suggestions during my long academic, journalistic, and corporate career.